THE PESSOA CHRONICLES

THE PESSOA

CHRONICLES

Poems, 1980-2016

George Monteiro

BRICKTOP

2016

Bricktop Hill Books
PO Box 1016
Willimantic, CT 06226

Library of Congress Control Number: 2016936474

ISBN 978-0-9973669-1-4

ISBN 0-9973669-1-5

To Bricktop Hill Books, my publisher,
who generously and courageously
took on this book.

Preface

Beginnings are apt to be shadowy, as Rachel Carson reminds us in *Silent Spring*. *The Pessoa Chronicles*—a collection, a scrap-book, an accumulation, an offering, take your pick—had its beginning as a *book*, as far as I can recall, around 1990 when, out of sheer curiosity, I culled from my files those poems that had to do with some aspect of Fernando Pessoa's life or work, and was surprised to find the number of them was greater than I had thought. It was then that I decided to gather into a single file what I began to call my "Pessoa poems," thinking that, as time went on, I might add a few more to the accumulation. Later on, I began to write poems meant expressly for the book. Some of the entries in *The Pessoa Chronicles* are expressed in the (imagined) voice of Pessoa speaking for himself or that of one or another of his heteronyms. Many others are in an unidentified voice, usually indistinguishable from mine. Following each entry is the date or dates when the lines were first set down. This dating, I must confess, serves also a personal and somewhat selfish purpose. The dates serve to remind me of what the weather was like for me, so to speak, by reminding me of what was on my mind on particular days in specific years. As such, the collection works for me as something of an autobiography—limited though it be, and given that purpose, although tempted as I was to do so, I rejected the idea of publishing a selection comprised of those items selected in accordance with my taste in 2016. And of course, as Dylan says, "Ah, but I was so much older then. I'm younger than that now."

A word about Fernando Pessoa. Born in Lisbon on June 13, 1888, he died in Lisbon, at the age of forty-seven, on

November 30, 1935. His formative years, however, were spent in Durban, the southern African city, where his stepfather served as Portuguese Consul. His formal education, except for a short time at the University of Lisbon, was entirely English. During his lifetime, though he contributed poems and letters to newspapers and journals in the major Portuguese cities, he managed to publish in separate form only a small handful of *plaquettes* comprised of poems in English and distributed exclusively in the British isles, and *Mensagem* (1934), a collection in Portuguese of Pessoa's largely ironic historical poems.

One of the great European Modernists of the twentieth century, Pessoa is now famous as the creator of heteronyms (what one may call alter egos or alter voices), for whom he devised detailed biographies, as well as distinctively different bodies of work. Three of them—Alberto Caeiro, Ricardo Reis, and Álvaro de Campos—have attained such individual reality that they have been recognized as "persons" in Portuguese literary history and given their own separate space in poetry anthologies. Pessoa's other great success is *Livro do Desasso-ssego*, a storehouse of prose fragments attributed to Bernardo Soares (a semi-heteronym) and cobbled together by his editors in various publishable forms long after Pessoa's death.

Contents

Preface

1980-1989

1980-1989

Surface Noise

It scares me, this life
I can't face up to. In
fact, while I can't
entirely bring it off, I
do better facing it down.
I'm an aggressive son-
of-a-bitch, but it's a
touch-and-go existence
I allow myself. Or is it
the touch-and-go myself
that allows the other—
the me I am—this,
and only this much?
Who speaks for me now
or through me? Is it
Fernando Pessoa, his
orthonymic self, sporting
with me, or is it one
of his sweaty heteronyms
scraping out a horned-bottom
scapegoat, who can't, or
won't, cry foul?

July 11, 1980

Filling In

The street
called Álvaro
de Campos
does not exist.
The street Álvaro
Castro does.
What does it matter
that Álvaro de
Campos' poetry
breathes today,
while Álvaro
Castro's does
not? The cab
drivers, who
should know
better, have not
yet learned to
admit that
they care.

July 13, 1980

Elegy for Temudo

When Fernando Pessoa died,
did he really think that he would
have followers, other than those
he had mesmerized (the presença
bunch) or those who had fallen

into his familial web, like Jorge de
Sena (a lucky catch, surely, but no
one could have said so at the time)?
Of course he didn't. At least not
when his brain was screwed securely
into his saucy skull. Well, tell him now,
those who think they can, that he did.
He had one unwitting follower across
the Atlantic, for example, who fancied
himself into three people in a composite
self-portrait and then entertained guests
by blossoming, before their eyes, into
a fourth personage ready to comment
on the three projections fixed softly
into a purpled-white photograph. Pessoa
did it best, but he didn't do it alone.

July 13, 1980

Many? Any?

How many poems
did Pessoa write
on the table-cloth
paper of the Café
Três Montanhas?
None, of course;
they had cloth
tablecloths, or,
at worse, none
at all. So, the old

sucker came prepared,
pen and paper in
pocket so that he
could impress the
habitués whether
he had a poem
perking or merely
bent low to fake it.

July 14, 1980

Almada's Pessoa

It's a canny picture.
The Master *in situ*,
suited up in black,
white-shirted, black-
tied, sits not straight,
but slightly over the
table, inclined to
the left (to the right
in the other), legs
crossed at the ankles.
He holds a cigarette
in one hand, while
the fingers of the
other hand rest firmly
on a rectangle of
purple paper. His pen
—is it his?—lies free
at the upper corner

of the paper. A coffee
cup, spoon in saucer,
and a sugar bowl sit
next to books. The
one on top is a copy
of *Orpheu 2*. The
subject wears a hat;
it too is black. Chair
and table match.
This, against a red
and gold and burnt
orange arrangement
of squares. There is
no cloth over the table,
not even a paper one
good for notes, poems,
notes for poems, or
minor calculations.
There is no booze:
no brandy, none of
the red. And if that
purple paper harbors
poetry, it does so on
the surface we don't see.
Campos/Reis/Caeiro
are not in the picture.

July 27 / Aug. 10, 1980

People

Of course Fernando Pessoa,
orphaned and then so-officially
adopted, set some wily goals
for himself. Tricked by his
Portuguese nativity, angered
at his needy mother, at his
good-marriage stepfather,
at his too-eager English-
language masters in Durban,
and burned to a curse, the man
wound his babies up and set
them free to make his way
in a regardless world.

Jan. 29, 1981

Honig's Pessoa

On the sly, out of Holland, comes the charge:
Honig's Pessoa misfires; henceforth despise
the man, banish his book, expunge his getting
the Master's best words to breathe in English.

White out the tumbling cat, the child eating
chocolates in the street. Slash away at the
randy frolics of *Maritime Ode*. Nail the New
World poet, learning his poet's Portuguese

here-and-there, getting it by bits and pieces,
securing the idiom as best he can. No matter
that Karl Shapiro, who knows no Portuguese,
hailed this Pessoa with gusto, an old boy up

there with Homer. No matter that a "Cornhusker
of the Year" thinks on the money Honig's turn
of phrase and enviable looping. No matter that
Jorge de Sena knows the Minotaur, like every-

body else, has no Portuguese. No matter that
Keats bobbled Balboa's discovery. No matter,
too, that the Dutch chap's translator matches his
client's malice in a language everybody knows.

Apr. 23, 1982

Clerking

My hand, too, is in the service of clarity—
like Fernando's. I, too, am a clerk with

business experience he cannot leave
behind. Clerks have always been writers

in the service of others, as he well knew.
But not all writers have been clerks,

which is why it's certain *ele-mesmo* did
the writing that the others would not do.

May 1, 1984

Almada's Pessoa (2)

I meet you here, in the museum,
larger than life, one centimeter

less that the 1.75 with which you
gifted Álvaro. Below the table you

are a dancer, a Pierrot. Above it
you are a *maître d'* on break or

a translator, perhaps, stopping off
on his way to work, to take a cup

of coffee and, as is your wont, to
spend a moment blowing smoke.

June 19, 1984

Costa Pinheiro's Pessoa

Chess pieces—king–sized pawns sitting like curates
in an Italian comedy.

The man himself dreams these other men who also dream
their sometimes technicolor dream to themselves.

These pieces while away the time, waiting to be taken, waiting
for ships that sail, women who stare, palm trees that stand.

All things are still—on the wing.

June 19, 1984

Location, Location

Almada owns, right now, the first room
—a large foyer—of the exhibiting area
of the shiny new Centro de Arte Moderna.

Never mind the trifles on the back wall
to the left as you enter. Take a good look
at what's on the facing walls, running left

and right, into the main room housing what
is permanent of the "others" (among whom
Almada surely numbers). But glance back

into the foyer, see his African tapestries, a
double triptych, scenes of immigration
(including a steerage one) paired with those

of a Lisbon Sunday, *cidade alfacinha* busy
at play. Many faces and many torsos and
limbs show forth in woven panels. Facing

them, on the right wall, there sits at a table,
in a belated work big with design, the messenger.
This canvas, Almada's deviant clone (no secret),

might affront these colorful carpets. But no, the
person in it doesn't look out of his clean space, so
clean that you can't see the smoke he has exhaled.

Imagined to a T, his people know less of Almada's
splendid, niggard world, having come to their own
realization only by way of balloons spoken in zeal.

July 4, 1984

Portuguese Letters

In the love letters of Fernando and Ophelia
(she's 19, he's 31) the *xi-coração* surprises
when it rears its corny head. I wince at this
word out of the child's world used to hold
at bay lovers heating up to consummate.

Jan. 10, 1985

Costa Pinheiro's Pessoa (2)

king / pawns
curates
in an Italian
movie

a man himself
dreams
unwise men who
themselves dream
ships that sail
standing palms
women staring
gulls
on the wing

Feb. 2, 1985

Bread Alone

Welcome speeches are delivered amid
bunches of cut flowers set out to

punctuate the proper positioning of
speakers. They do not live by Pessoa

alone. Yet who is there among us to
separate the shepherd from his sheep?

Dec. 1, 1985

The Winner Speaks

Well, the poem wasn't that good, I guess,
and it probably isn't that bad, either.
Who knows? Nobody, I know, can say

either way since my prize-winning book
in 1934 has no readers. How sad, now,
that its author, a half-century later,
apologizes for winning—no, that's not
right—apologizes for his competitor's
not winning the prize. Actually the jury
liked it, I say, but it wasn't long enough;
it fell well short of the required one
hundred pages, no matter how much
blank space they left on the page and
between sections. So they gave it a
second prize—not, let's be clear about this,
the second prize (which, of course, was not
provided for in the regulations; you can look
them up). What a way to live one's life. Win
a prize and for the next fifty years hear
the good things said only about what many
still consider to be the runner-up (though
there shouldn't have been one of those,
as I, Vasco Reis, have already said).

Dec. 24, 1985

On the Money

Sérgio on the 5000 escudo bank-
note looks like Pessoa, affluent,
selling confidence, branching out.
Yet Pessoa, on the 100 escudo bill
can hardly be said to favor Sérgio.

Think of it as a sort of holograph,
sometimes this, sometimes that.

June 13, 1986

Anniversary

Today I'd be ninety-eight if not for the drink, the kidney
shutdown, and God knows what else that put me away before
my time.

My remains—all that lived at the old address—have now been
whisked away to Jerónimos.

Life's like that. Just when it all seems settled—once and for
all—you up and move or somebody does the moving for you.
To live to ninety-eight, now that's going too far, but seventy or
seventy-five, that's o.k.

What a chest I'd have left you. A fleet of chests, all of them
filled with bits and pieces, things and puzzles that would amuse
you for a century, nay, a millennium.

I would have preferred but one interment, when memory itself
was fresh, rosy, green.

June 13, 1986

Mnemosyne

The old woman plunks herself down
next to us at the first of the three marble-
top tables set in rows in *A Brasileira*.

She would talk, taking us for somebody
who might talk back. Anything, to make
her day for only a little bit. Finally Antonio

responds to her overture, the last of many.
She comes here often, as well as every
other place in the neighborhood. Are we

painters? No? No matter. She'll talk to us
anyway. She's old, very old, but lively,
even frenetic. We guess her age. She's

seventy-seven. Only seventy-seven, I say
to myself, and yet, and yet. Did she come
here today to celebrate his birthday? Did

she know him? I don't ask these questions.
But there's no sign whatever of Himself. It's
a holiday in Lisbon; he must be out of town.

June 13, 1986

His Temerity

What is hard to impress on strangers
is that, except for his reserve, he was
one of the crowd. Top coat, well-turned
brim, cigarette, glasses gave him solidity.
His smoke curled over reality's things,
places. His poems dream rings around
the merry-go-round he walked every day.

June 18, 1986

Parthenogenesis

One, two, three, born
just like that, each his

own man, all internal
network loyalties not

withstanding, Reis,
Caeiro, Campos—a

hat trick if there ever
was one, profligacy

indeed for a poet who
owned no more than

one hat—never black—
at any given moment.

June 20, 1986

Advantage

He, the only poet (but he, at the least, four
of them) with a clean look at the courtyard,
looks out at cameras and lights set up for
an evening performance by Carlos Paredes.

It's a very small stand, and around the marker
along the stones flooring the alcove rest
technicians' boxes, tools and wires and other
needful things. It is convenient to house it

all there, out of the airy passageways, away from
the cameras. Of these things the poet will speak
in his own good language, to the happy few.

June 20, 1986

Comparative Literature

Odd coincidence that both of them
should have lived, at one or another
time, on Ridge Road, though one
such address was in Durban, at the
tip (bottom or top) of Africa, the

other in pedestrian Rutherford (in
even more pedestrian) New Jersey.
One was a decade-long place to live
in, the other a rest-of-one's life
place-of-business, house to live in,
to die in. Almost the same age,
these stay-at-home poets labored
at their trades, forms of translation
engaged in by the pediatrician and
by the writer of commercial letters
in foreign tongues; match them,
waxing poetic: one *Ode Maritima*
for a *Paterson*, or one *Spring and
All* for all of Álvaro de Campos'
sweetly bilious bursts of verse.
Oh, by the way, for a time the
peregrinating Pole Czeslaw
Milosz signed out of Ridge
Road, Berkeley, California.

June 30, 1986

Being Thomas Crosse

Off-handedly, almost, Pessoa
told a correspondent that his

attempts, the night before, to
think up paradoxes had come

to nothing worth talking about—
the evidence that scratching

lit a fuse that scorched straight
through the surface of his soul.

Oct. 1, 1987

Fire in the Chiado

Tend to that little spot of fire in the timbers, dry
and festive, deep in the structure of the Grandola
until the flame is supple enough to run courses
in three directions: down left and right and up
straight ahead. Burn up everything, left and right,
along both sides of the cobble-stone streets. But,
also, burn not, as a matter of course, the Livraria
Bertrand, that long-ago publisher of Gaspar Simões'
life-and-work volumes on the poet. Spare, as well,
the other bookstore, all innocent in what's important.
Spare, too, the village church, and, of course, the
Largo de S. Carlos and *A Brasileira*, places dear to
my imagination. The sitting poet, a failed copy of
James Michael Curley, sitting hard by Faneuil Hall,
can go—or stay—I care not. Just think, by the way,
of the TAP steward who, knowing both figures, told
me he prefers, rightly, Boston's. So far, I fear, the
likeness on the 100 escudo note takes the cake.

Jan. 6, 1988

Yorick

Well, they've done it.
They have conflated
the messenger with
the messiah and have
charged him with
all the responsibility.
What a fool! What
a poor, sentimental,
backward-looking
futurologist, promising
the Fifth Empire, this
word-person who
couldn't elaborate
his *Faust* beyond
the fragments that
shored up nothing,
that sustained and
fed only the poet's
guilt before his
unfinished opus.
But the message,
the message. Never
mind the messenger
or the messiah.

Mar. 25, 1988

The Good Doctor Speaks

In this place, the Vera Cruz of the ancients, where
I followed my trade as best I could and wrote my
best and good poems (throwing away the rest),
they hold their conference, but they do not pay

any special homage to me. Even the author of an
account of my brief existence after the close of
the Master's life chooses to talk about his own work
and his vocation rather than my modest, yet more

than competent, poems, poems that he once took
to be the expression, oddly, of what he calls a "real"
person. It is not betrayal I feel, not exactly. It's more
like the pressure of sadness felt like heavy engulfing

air that breaks one down and down into a form, meta-
phorically, of the temporary and temporizing bends.
Waiting too long is all of that and nothing else matters.

Oh blessed Lear, who chose even the dead-wrong
action over the long, slow wait for fairness or love.

Apr. 30, 1988

The Proper Positioning

Who the hell is this guy,
hard as metal, sitting
outside twenty-four

hours a day, subject
to rain and bird-shit,
fair game to any sunny
son-of-a-bitch who will
put up with his stupid
silence? He is a dumb
polyglot, arm lifted in
the air as if he is about
to punctuate a thought.
Do not believe it. He's
just been caught rolling
his haunches. Looky.

July 25, 1988

Sailor Suit, Whistle and Cigarette

His mother's child, deprived
of his primacy (he thought),

made up friends to throw
up against his stepfather,

the Consul. It worked so
well he continued to people

his life with friends but
couldn't even tolerate them

all alive so he made them up
dead (well, only some of them).

Bad, bad boy, always day-
dreaming, and worse, writing

things down.   Stuff fit for spit-
balls, but no classroom to

throw them in. No mums, no
stepdaddy, no *tia*, no boss,

no voice to tell him no, to see
that he face reality, to recognize

that no one was there to pick up
the pieces when the drunk went

smash and the fantasies went
the way of all airy things.

Nov. 14, 1988

English Poet

The boy who did not know
he could not write a passable
English poem egregiously
and madly fiddled away at
his Anglo-Saxon task.

Why blossom, you ask
him, to blow, blush unseen,
and fade away before

disdainful strangers?
Just a miscalculation.

Nov. 14, 1988

Pessoana

What do I care
about all this
stuff about him,
if I understand
him well enough
and need only a
guide or two?
What do I care
about this hired
gun who tolerates
nothing other
than what she
thinks she sees?

Basta. Let's put
an end to all this
dopey talk about
dialogue. Let's
work alone and
abandon this
darkness spun

out in concert
with others.

Nov. 14, 1988

Romaria in New Orleans

Well, he didn't deserve
a second prize, either.
Antonio Ferro's son,
privy to the encoded
messages, reveals them
now to a smaller audience.
Portugal, Portugal, Portugal.
The myth that is everything
is the myth that is nothing.
Here we see the first bubble
of a new birth of the old,
now very old *Estado Novo*.

Nov. 18, 1988

Samarra

I see Angel in the street in
the Baixa and I remember
how I announced his death
on another continent at

another time. I greet him
and he, confused but affable
as ever, thanks me—
inappropriately. How

cherubic this ageing, pipe-
sucking poet-scholar, I
think after the fact. How
alive and kicking this man

who knows not how I bruited
about the rumor that he was
dead but now seems to know
something he cannot tell.

Dec. 8, 1988

At Work

Pomar has put him aplenty in the subway
and now those who ride by or those who
merely wait can all look at *ele-mesmo*

reading a newspaper as he gets a shine.
For anyone on the move, in or out, there
he be, an indicator of every which way.

Dec. 11, 1988

1990-1999

Campos Records a Death

Hanging still from the festering
vine, the playboy shuts down
his high-wire act for his friend

back in Lisbon, for the few of
Orpheu, eager to bark their
applause, ever anxious to bite.

It's no longer seemly to run in
place, with drafts from Africa a
thing of the past. He has plans;

no, a plan. Once, twice, three
times he hesitates, and tables.
When a fourth chance presents

itself, propitious to the moment
down to the minute, he strikes,
and with the trick accomplished,

fulfills his fate: discoloring—
bloating—bursting buttons.
His hat sits on a chair. Then—

poof—it vanishes, along with
a dead man's trunk, hotel-held
for room-rent, due and unpaid.

Crazy for the singular rose,
the tart lives on, merely in regret
for her out-of-pocket luxuries.

May 19, 1990

Hemispheric Pressures

He could not have written Frost's *Road
Not Taken*. One of his heteronyms could
have, but their progenitor could not have,
since with them, he walked down all the
roads he cared to walk. It's odd that the
American wrote his poem in the same year
that, in Lisbon, the poet's inexistent coterie
first made the primal scene in his bedroom.

June 1, 1990

Starts

Nothing in this life lasts
like the memory of pain.

Well, that's out of the way.

A child walks her addled grand-
mother up the Rua Garrett.
The old woman screams.

The mayor might authorize
a census of the uses to which
the citizenry put the poet's statue.
A man in black, for instance, even
as I speak, offers him a bite of cold
French toast fresh from *A Brasileira*.
A young woman pats his arm, then
his hat. Nobody spits in his face.

Here, too, young black men move
in packs.

Like theirs, his genius expects
recognition.

Jan. 6, 1991

Beggar, Book, and Radio

In the Chiado some of the beggars
read at their stations, usually in
the warmth of direct sunlight.
Before the church of the martyrs

one of them listens to the game,
a cigarette glued to his lower lip.
The days these people put in, day-
in-day-out, are long and tedious.

(I wrote this poem ten years ago,
and it was better, truer, then.)

An old guy sits in the chair next
to Pessoa, open-mouthed (maybe

diabetic), the sounds of the game
coming from the radio he holds
up between himself and—an
accommodation—the sitting poet.

Jan. 11, 1991

Politics and Ideology

The maids in Lisbon hotels do not speak
Pessoa's language, as my friend claimed.

Doubtlessly, he was misinformed by his
friend who, after all, might only have been

passing on someone else's fancy notion.
The maids of the Hotel Dom Carlos in 1991

harry one another in tried and true fish-wife
style, while speaking their subdued good

mornings to their serviced clientele on their
way down to breakfast. But their trade makes

them wily, as they learn in a blinking minute
a stranger's habits, perfected over a lifetime.

Jan. 11, 1991

Reprise

Tell me Fernando, if you can, why bother with a narrative if
the payoff is to knock off a poet, eased into being, ode by ode.

Apr. 23, 1991

Of March 8, 1914

He told a tall story
studded with facts,

dates, names—of
standing at a high

chest to glean his
populous brain and

the poems came
tumbling out like

fraternity boys out
of a phone booth

or a funny family
deserting a VW.

An ant farm; a
beehive droning

away unbeknownst
to its keeper, an

untrained shepherd
counting his thoughts

to keep awake for
the first time, all

parts of speech to be
and therefore to differ.

July 6, 1991

Once More

In a couple of hours or so it's
your birthday. I sit before

the Palácio Nacional. Lovers
make out in cars while old

men parade their intentions.
The young poet befriended

by Sylvia at the beginning
of his English life elevates

into his episcopacy (there's
smoke, and faded colors)—

and I am off in Sintra where
the youngest Sena girl stands

in a doorway, watching, judging
nothing, judging everything.

June 12, 1992

Non-Campos in Sintra

Álvaro is still on the road
but I'm in the dark, hunting
and pecking at this radio
shack implement. Is all of
this worth it, the *blague*,
the poppycock about souls
—mean and not so mean?

June 13, 1992

Martinho da Arcada

Of course he would not come here now.
The prices, comparatively speaking, are
out of sight, and speaking of sight, it is not
likely that he would willingly take the walk
of an afternoon back to his day, given the
traffic and the ordinary good manners of
the Lisbon citizenry. Bad paintings infest

the walls, too. It's enough to make a man
give up drink or do his drinking at home.

June 15, 1992

Couvert?

He's fat and old—at one
hundred and four. You'd
not know him, his having
given up his eyeglasses
for soft contacts, and now
saying he's on the wagon—
almost. He still gulps it
down from the customer's
glass he carries back to
the washer. Of course
I'm making this up—
about the drinking and
non-drinking, too, for I
simply don't know. Truth
is, the old Ibis was never
above doing any of this.

June 15, 1992

Pomar's Choice

Why choose,
for Pomar's

series of Pessoa,
Alto dos Moinhos,
a metro station
so far from the
man's habits and
haunts? Rhetorical
question, this, to
the *ibero*.

Sept. 9, 1993

Casa Fernando Pessoa

The outreach in this poet's house
occurs on the top floor where set up

and running is a slide projector that
throws rapid skips of light but no image

onto a blank wall. The light goes out
even as I write, but the mechanism

continues to hum, running through
its strangely quiet noisy functions.

Dec. 7, 1993

Choices

Within sight of Fernando's
last domicile, at Rua Coelho
da Rocha, 16, is a small public

square featuring a green bronze
bust of the *Duque de Wellington
(1769-1852)*. Fronting the square

is the British Hospital. All this,
less than 100 meters from F. P.'s
house and readily seen from its

front windows. He himself must
have sat in this small four-benched
square. Odd that he must die in the

French hospital, after having lived
a fictional life that was, in certain
senses, all but exclusively English.

Dec. 7, 1993

Keeping the Poet Informed

From the office at the Casa Fernando
Pessoa comes the voice of a clerk who
tells of over-hearing in the street, as she
returned from lunch, the boast of one who

prevented a fight by hugging one of the
gajos so hard that she cracked his ribs.

Dec. 7, 1993

Santiago de Compostela

1. At the Catedral de Santiago de
Compostela, in an open book on
display in the library, in the middle
of the page, Federico García Lorca

has signed in. It is 1916 and he
is eighteen. Above his signature,
there is a statement, signed properly,
respectfully. And now there are

many other signatures below his or
on the facing page. This was not a
competition but he has won out.
From the encased book, names that

are long forgotten surround the
fancied star of death and fame.
All else is buried thick, page upon
page, seldom turned to purpose.

2. At the great Cathedral
mass begins, but priests
keep arriving late, and in
the end there are many priests.

One of them, after a bit,
limps off the set, another
follows him, each one
having done his part.

I'm too cool to hug the Saint.
Some of the huggers I'm watching
are better at the hugging thing
than others. Some merely touch,

one hand; some pat, consolingly;
some enjoy a good feel. Then I,
too, hug the Saint. I'm surprised
to find him cold. It's not the cold

that kills, but it chills. In the
Cathedral men confess face-to-
face; women, on the other hand,
their faces off to the side.

The open square opens out to greet
this Englishman's voice. belting
out show tunes. He accepts small
monies, with pride, warmth, fealty.

3. It's the same everywhere
I go, the world does not
stand at attention. Lives
drift or drive along, the sun

shines or it does not, and
only a few pilgrims recall

while the rest of the world
forgets to care or simply

be aware. Amherst largely
nods, Hartford continues
to close down, and Padrón
builds its factory across

the tracks running before
the grapes shading the walls
and table and the one seat
with a back—all is made of

stone—at the house of
Rosalia, Padrón's poet.
At this moment all this

world's attention depends
on me, I think, but that—
that surely must be wrong.

Oct. 9 / 10, 1994

I Suppose I Shouldn't Be

I am glad that Fernando Pessoa never had to mow
the lawn or put out the rubbish or scramble eggs
of a Sunday morning.

After all, he was a poet and a thinker and a worker,
though a sad-sack screw-up in what most of us would
call life.

Better to walk in the shade of the *arcada* to the Martinho
for some *tinto* or pre-prandial cognac than to weed
a garden or pray for rain.

He would have left us the same messages and probably
even more fragments of disquietude but might have been
a mite happier or, at the least, more worldly productive.

Foolish questions, fond thoughts, for he was always busy
with worry (for himself and the others) playing poetry
to the hilt and dreading the rain.

Aug. 7, 1995

The Benoits

I've taken to looking for Benoits
first thing in the *New Yorker,*
right out of the mailbox
sometimes even, when it isn't

raining, on the way back to the
house. The spot drawings are
my quarry, the search for the
signs of Pessoa, who was at first

named but lately just there,
like identity-blind stamps,
unnamed, unidentified,
anonymous, icons—a book,

eyeglasses, a drink—with
a secret source, a hidden
significance—perhaps signs
cut adrift from their reference.

Bottles with no message to
be fished out of harbors,
no pizza for the tenth caller,
no candy for the sweet-tooth.

Oct. 4, 1995

Three on a Match

Pessoa's naval engineer was trained at the Univ. of Glasgow.
While precise dates of his time there have gone unrecorded,
the fact that he was born in 1890 makes it that his studies date
from the early to mid-years of the second decade of the 20th
century. As luck would have it, on Nov. 30, the very day his
(virtual) progenitor died in Lisbon, John Drew Cormack, a
retired professor of engineering at the Univ. of Glasgow, also
died. Cormack was Fernando Pessoa's senior by 18 years
and Álvaro de Campos' by 20. In her *Foto-biografia* Maria
José de Lancastre does not mention John Drew Cormack
but offers a photograph captioned, a bit cheekily: *Glasgow,*

onde Álvaro de Campos estudou engenharia. Rumor has it
that Campos died (before his time) on November 30, 1935.

Nov. 30, 1995

Cascais, *Jamais*

Whatever made him think he would do?
Politics apart, he should have filled the
bill, the slightly startled, ever vigilant,
ever suspicious mien of the birdlike clerk
he encountered at Cascais had no more
need of him than he, after all, of Cascais.

Feb. 2, 1996

On His Way

To my great surprise,
walking down from above,
I fail to meet the poet.
Fully expecting to come
upon him, I go right
by *A Brasileira*, thinking
I'm still not there. He's
gone. Metro works are
underway, right where
he's sat, it now seems,
forever. Gone. I imagine
things. He just up and left

one moonless night, having
heard the rumors, and lurks
now in the old homestead
in the Largo de S. Carlos.
Or, on a sunny afternoon,
workmen enticed him with
the promise of a closer look
at the Tejo, even a saunter
down to the Cais de Sodré,
only to shanghai him into a
van straight to the old PIDE
headquarters a mere street
or two away. Or (I like this
one best) the Pope sent for
him and he now, ensconced
in his chair as is his custom,
rides perpetually, in his own,
unshared *pessoa*-mobile, on
his way to London, at last.

Apr. 20, 1996

Half-Gods

Casais Monteiro worried rings around his Master. Pessimism
—his—struck others like friendly fire, a low-toned bombing
that laid siege to citadels of happy whistling.

Steadily and slowly he worked his vein of iron well beyond the
comforts of a handy, all-purpose *saudades*. (That's for others,

who, in a pinch, can always call on their *saudades* for *saudade* itself.)

Casais Monteiro had an attitude. He rested nowhere, he cared for nothing he had or could ever dream of having—not solitude, not peace, not place or friend, not love or even the love of love. He was grumpy, grumpy in spades.

Apr. 21, 1996

Trilby

Smaller than life
but larger than death,
this personal poet
faked a temperament,
denied reality, accepted
(too easily) his nothingness.
He was not courageous
but was fearful and agile,
a stick figure in a black suit,
a fedora, and a gabardine—
all to set off his umbrella,
his wire-rimmed glasses,
his pretense that puppets
pulled his strings.

June 7, 1996

Foolish Boy

What made him think he'd pass
muster as a librarian? Pushing
his luck (and too-trusting of his
literary reputation), he sent off
his c.v. and settled back on his
haunches. But the sinecure went
elsewhere, to the other applicant.

Why? you ask. Well, speculate.
He lived in Lisbon (they knew he
wouldn't always make it up the
coast), he drank too much (he'd be
too far from his suppliers), and—
the last straw—it was widely known
that he wrote all over his papers.

Sept. 26, 1996

Pomar's Imaginary

For the metro, in *azulejo* Pomar sets
him forward, off on his haunches,
leaning over, getting his shoes shined.
Being so excellently served, for a coin,
gives him that warm feeling that comes
only with the rag-snap of a good shine.

Jan. 12, 1997

Prazeres

Let's face it. There's no
pleasure for him in this
place. Even the cemetery
with the cheeky name is a
thing of the past. Now that
Angel Crespo, too, has
disappeared I place my hands—
having set down my pad— on
this black-on-black monument,
seeking out heat, hoping to
replicate the Spanish feat.
                No heat, no heat,
less heat, no, no heat, as my
hands move from stone to metal,
and back to stone, until at the last
I think I sense something, a trace,
hardly a flash. I pick up my pad.
                His coterie of three
finds itself quoted here, but not
himself, having had silence
chosen for him.
                But it's not too late,
surely, for a signal from the surface
hidden away from the garden, say,
or the blank stare, something
for the nonce, at the least.

Jan. 12, 1997

Bernardo Soares at Rest

He has his lunch on the Rua dos
Douradores (Restaurante Pessoa).

It need not be a special occasion,
though costing a trifle more than

he wants to pay every day, but
here he comes, finding it piquant

to eat in somebody's eponymous
place, especially when the presence

of his quirky friend makes it less lonely
to be by himself. Sena sits here today,

older than he will ever become but
looking healthy, no evidence, in sight,

of heart attack or cancer. He reads
a newspaper, after wine, dessert and

coffee. I see Severino, talking away to
a friend, wearing no shades, his eyes

are still reasonably good. I look about.
There's no one else here, no one I know.

I do not notice when the assistant to the
bookkeeper goes out, back to his numbers.

Jan. 13, 1997

Misprision

Falta-me limar os versos,
said one of my cohort.
Me? I just file them
away. Well, that's not
so, strictly speaking.
Actually the scraps on
which I have scribbled
I religiously lay to rest
atop the accumulation,
a sludge pile I intend
to sort out later on.

June 13, 1997

Tea Leaves

It cannot be imagined: Pessoa
crying out in pain or yelling in
anger. Despite the pictures of
him on the move through the
lower city, the thought of him
reacting spontaneously in time
to time's tireless coursing

cannot be sustained. Time drifts,
but not for him, despite what
he says, and he says plenty.

Apr. 19, 1998

Delegation

Like Hamlet with Ophelia,
when he wanted to distance

himself from her, Fernando
feigned madness. He had

Álvaro de Campos give her
the stunning news—in a letter,

of course. And if his Ophelia
did not drown herself or enter

a nunnery, she did not marry
until Fernandinho was dead.

Dec. 7, 1998

Don't Mind if I Do

The tables all taken
and every seat filled,
this tourist with a book

—in hardcover—
sits in the chair next
to the poet (who, as
always, looks away).
There's no sound
emanating from this
monument of brass
save the noise from
fleshy lips that move
slowly across a page.
The poet sits along.

Dec. 7, 1998

Lisboa (1972-1998)

I've tried very hard
to make this my city.

I've walked the same
few walks, I've risen

from the same metro
stations, I've slowly

acquired new places,
new restaurants,

or what have you—
It's not, it's not yet,

nor is it likely to be.
There's no heat for

me in Jerónimos at
the Pessoa stone.

Dec. 8, 1998

Well, There's a Crane

hanging high over the birthplace,
and the mural parading Almada's

characters is covered, except for
the figure of Caeiro, who must

oversee the refurbishing, I take it,
employed gainfully for once.

Dec. 9, 1998

Twelfth Night in the Chiado

The best place for skateboarding is
the nearest hill to the concrete runway
built to bring people up to the Chiado
after the fire. Just above it pretty and

not-so-pretty women take turns sitting
alongside the poet for their pictures.
This one touches his firm hand—but
too late—the gesture won't be in the

picture. Many people, usually of a
certain age, mind authority's business.
An open gate to an empty lot evokes
righteous annoyance. A woman

bubbles imprecations angrily at my
host's decision to park the wrong way
on the street. Live and let live? No.
 "But his work is so important you

can read him in German," speaks
the man to her, in perfect English,
before it can be used for poetry—
Pessoa expands on the Lake Poet.

I sit on a bench before A Brasileira
and I don't understand all this any
better than I would, were I standing
tall, ready to face the task before me.

Jan. 6, 1999

Network

With Caeiro dead
& Álvaro too quick

on the trigger for
his acquired taste,
only himself would
do. But there are
no letters, none
between Ricardo
and his enabler,
or between either
of them and the
Brazilian rep of
of the short-lived
Orpheu. Ronald
de Carvalho could
have as a matter
of course placed
his verse, intro'd
him around Rio,
referred patients.
But nothing. Only
silence from the
land of the *pau-*
brasil, the island
of Vera Cruz—
then Saramago.

May 16, 1999

Who? Where? When?

Who can spot the ringer?
In a crowd there are many,

but alone he defies detection
by being himself, that is,
being just like everyone
else. It is said that the one
who was the extraordinary
poet Elizabeth Bishop lived
out her life impersonating a
perfectly ordinary middle-
class woman, though she
fooled no one, not even
the help.

May 23, 1999

2000-2009

Sleeping Dogs

> *Os restos mortais de Luís de Camões*
> *não estão nunca estiveram aqui foram,*
> *secretamente sepultados no cemitério*
> *dos prazeres sob o heterònimo de*
> *Fernando Pessoa.*
> José Paulo Paes, *Mosteiro*
> *dos Jerônimos*

Not so, not so, I say; but if so,
they're back again, for once.

Yet Shapiro has a point, too,
when he devotes his poem

to the triple tomb honoring
the enshrined modern Master.

The voices he voices are
the voices of Caeiro, Reis,

and Campos—nothing, but
nothing, emanating from

F. P. himself. Of course
no one can find anywhere

what's not there to begin
with. So only the three.

When they took their
pleasure in digging up

the bones in the grave
at *Prazeres*, did they

actually get their man
or were such remains

those of some mute
inglorious person taken

unexpectedly on a joy
ride to please the nags

of the city? As for Him-
self, he's sitting pretty;

he's the M.I.A., purloined
corpse of the Chiado.

Jan. 26, 2000

Caeiro, Be Not Proud

Having hit on your one truth, you
bid fair to become a grotesque,

scattering angels and gargoyles
and sundry folk of the air to make
space do your bidding, to make it
yours alone in the midst of those
dumber or smarter than yourself.

Feb. 1, 2000

After Caeiro, What Forgiveness?

To believe in statistics is to live in
another, perhaps no less real world
than this one, but another world
nevertheless. To read this world
as a text, as an allegory of a world,
is to believe in still another world
indefinable except by its not being
this one. Knowledge takes up no
space, but then neither does illusion.

Feb. 2, 2000

After Class

To trace the Shakespearean spoor
through the poems of the dramatic

projection he himself called Álvaro
de Campos, calls for heavy-footed

sleuthing, announcing everything
as you go, partly to warn, to move

aside, partly to stake a claim
to acts made less real as you go.

Mar. 3, 2000

Bookman in São Paulo

He did not introduce me to Pessoa
but Sr. Jaime sold me my first Pessoa.
It was a second edition of Maria Aliete
Galhoz's Aguilar collection published
in Rio de Janeiro, ten years earlier.

He also sold me the *Páginas Íntimas*
and the *Páginas Estéticas*, volumes
that I wondered even then whether I
would ever peruse for pleasure let alone
read for work—the covers now heavy

with tape. He sold me other needful
things, such as dictionaries (I chose
the other set, not the *Melhoramentos*,
failing to catch, at the time, his polite
signals). He called his bookstore

Livraria 'Fernando Pessoa', but, as
far as I knew, there was no building,
no space to browse aimlessly or cruise

for bargains of that joyful nugget.
He was his bookstore, and *Livraria*

'Fernando Pessoa' went with him
wherever he went, open to the trade
when he set up shop between classes
outside the classrooms at the back
of the slapped-together, one-story

cement structures packed off in the
far corner of Cidade Universitária,
rumored to have been designed for
horses, germane to the Veterinary
School and destined to be turned

over to those very people who knew
how best to use the shacks. We called
them *galinheiros*, somehow the
right place for timid teachers and
their politically-cowed students.

Sr. Jaime sold his books on credit to
the students, who would otherwise
have had to travel well into the center
of the city of São Paulo to get their
books had he not faithfully, weekly,

trucked his hoard in to the *galinheiros*.
The last time I saw him he accommodated
me by searching through his hoard for
Jorge de Sena books. I disappointed him
when I bought only two or three of them

(I had copies of the others). I should have
bought every one of them. After all, can
anyone ever have enough Sena (or Pessoa),
crisp and very near mint duplicates, so
carefully accumulated, so providentially

stored away—awaiting scholars, ephebes,
neophytes—by one faithful enough to his
office to greet all those who, time and
again, visited this watering hole to satisfy
a thirst they didn't even know was theirs?

Mar. 6, 2000

The Gift

It is eighty-six years to the day
his troika came to him as he wrote

away atop a chest of drawers (or
so he claimed, twenty years later).

Pressed for an explanation of his
drama-em-gente, he invented a

narrative of narratives, an act of the
imagination that so far has sufficed.

Mar. 8, 2000

His Masque for One

The day was wet, cold, conducive to the third cognac
if he had any, which he didn't. The vertigo, familiar,

increasingly of late, was still unwelcome, though now
he didn't any longer think he need not go, if only to keep

to his horoscope's truth of at least another year to devote
to piecing shards into wholes, parts and parcels ordered

to an opus, smoke into things. No knocking at the gate,
no crone hawking flowers, no policemen on bicycles,

no whistling from the hired lookout, yet it had come—
removal from his street-facing bedroom to the Hospital

de S. Luís dos Franceses (ignoring the English hospital,
visible from his window, a stone's throw away), an odd

and de-familiarizing place, a place to set aside his glasses,
compose a sentence that would last, and breathe himself

out. What dream did he dream, this dreamer who dreamt
the poems of his time, the poems of dream, as uremic

poison coursed his body, suffused his brain, quenched
his endemic curiosity, taking him to last or first or new

thoughts? To-morrow brought him no new to-day, no
new surmises at sunrise, no visits to Abel's, no hang-

dog posturing at the end of day. Still a day late, and,
as ever, one last drink, a poem, and a paycheck short.

Apr. 20-21, 1999 / Jan. 16, 2001

Go Green

a figure 4,
weathered,
verdigris

May 10, 2001

Crossing on the D. João de Castro

He shall return tonight to his father's homeland via
TAP on a plane that's just been towed to Bay 53,
(International Departures) at the Newark airport.

Still state-owned, I think, these *caravelas* are named
for Bartolomeu Dias, Gama and the antsy Prince, a
navigator of personal ambition in the ships of others.

He shall return tonight to his mother's fatherland, to
the early light of the capital city, to Chiado bookstores,
to Baixa windows full of silver, rosé gold, *prata de lei*,

which, he will always be told (until he changes shoes),
is only marginally legal silver. This is not his fatherland, not
his motherland, and yet it is something to him, he, who cares

more for a safe flight surely than those sailors the Prince
sent out to stake claims and snatch riches, could have prayed
for—no matter where they had roamed.   It's all biography.

June 10, 2001.

A Sighting

Even an uncommon
talent for the periphery
will not enable him to

see his predecessor
staring down the main
artery of the Chiado.

Perhaps he glances at
the box of sea or ample
sky, bright blue, almost

cloudless, I imagine.
Perhaps not, for even
those eyes must one

time rest, unblinking,
at outdoor sleep. Just
thoughts, these, after

seeing an old postcard
of the Praça de Camões
at auction on e-bay.

Aug. 18, 2001

Super-Camões

That's him, standing
there, facing the statue

representing the poet
who gives the square

its name. Somewhat
heavier, seemingly,

than I'd have thought,
given the date of

the postcard. Still,
we'd all know him

anywhere. Just check
out the *pasta* under

his left arm, as he sizes
up the competition

for a moment, on his
way to the Baixa to

take up what another
might call his life.

Aug. 18, 2001

Ele-mesmo When Not Himself

When you have photos
like those of Fernando
on the fly, papers in hand,
feet barely striking
the pavement, the simple

mosaic of stones, why not
get a sculptor like Johnson
to catch him in the act of
being himself or not him-
self even (doesn't matter)?

Better this person on
his way to an appointment
or a drink than the brazenly
tall book, for a headless,
heedless Forest Gump,

blind to the river his brainless
body faces, a bookish reminder
that it should be easier to

navigate the seas than face
an omnivorous west.

Oct. 8, 2001

Oblique Rain

Well, they're missing, gone
from the wall running along
the Rua Paiva de Andrade,
Largo de S. Carlos side.
Who'd have thought it, that
the copies of Almada's figures
for the major players were
here only for the short haul?
Nor is the site, set in stone,
any longer a place to park cars.
*Mundial Confiança, Companhia
de Seguros*—new owners, new
tenants—swept clean, all of it.

Oct. 12, 2001

À mão esquerda

Two women,
traveling together,

purses strapped
to their backs,

take turns
photographing

one another sitting
with the poet.

One of them poses
with her hand on

the hand of the poet
(his left) resting

on the small table
next to him, not

in defiance, barely
a gesture.

Oct. 12, 2001

Columbus Day

It must be hell
sitting there, day
after day, in
the midst of tourists,
tables now to his
right and to the back,
tables in front of
him and down Rua

94

Garrett. It must be
hell for this private
man even in the midst
of publicity (which he
theorized). It's his fate
never to go home to
his books and his
papers, to be here
day and night for
the amusement of
strangers, never to
be swallowed back
into *A Brasileira*.

Oct. 12, 2001

Memento mori

Here, where death matters more
than birth, the poet's last domicile
is a museum, while his birthplace
is given over to selling insurance.

Jan. 9, 2002

Out in Front

It's January—a flute
works the paying
customers. A picture-

taker—film maker?
French? yes (to both)
—photographs a young
woman, speaking
American English.
He gets her to give him
a name and maybe an
address, at the edge
of the metro steps.
Nobody at the moment
attends to the sitting
poet. Then everything
starts up again—in
Portuguese this time
(or so it seems).

Jan. 9, 2002

How Alex Got to Durban

Sitting before his plate of boiled fish and
boiled potatoes and something green,

the whole suffused with olive oil, the scholar-
diplomat from Porto made the scholar

from Olhão an offer he didn't want himself:
represent the land of his birth at the 1988

centenary Pessoa celebration in Durban—
o.k. for an American, this tricky potato.

Alex said his slow yes, and I settled down
into second place, the never-to-be-asked.

July 3, 2002

Once Upon a Time

In the last churning months
preceding the Colonels' day

and the triumph of the long-
stemmed carnation, the fretful

doctor-folklorist in Oporto tells
me of the time he laid eyes on

the "so-called Master": "Small,
hunched over, sitting alone in the

far corner of a cheap bar—a mere
shadow of nothing." But memory

offers up, in its stead, Almada's dandy
—poised, engaged, deceitful.

Aug. 19, 2003

Cardoso Pires Has His Say

'Rain pouring, sadness growing,
and to ease the pain, the whiskey
flowing,' quote the denizens of the
Lisbon tavern. Still, Pessoa, who
knows the drill by heart, having
'decilitered' at bars all over Lisbon,
sits out on the esplanade in the rain
and, what's worse, without a drink.

Dec. 15, 2003

The Shill

It just won't do,
to let him sit there,

day after day, years
on end, and so on,

a Wal-Mart greeter,
too stoned to speak.

Sit with him, fittingly
at his left hand.

Antero would have
nodded in approval

or maybe chortled.
Take any two poles,

parallel them, place
them under his seat

and spirit him away
—pronto!

Dec. 17, 2003

The Long View

The day after Portugal's Golden
Generation of footballers loses
its first game in the Euros to the
contemptible Greeks, things in the
Chiado continue to surround but
not implicate the implacable Mr.
Person, his back to *A Brasileira*, a
modest recrimination to the Greeks,
in bronze (not stone), clothed, hatted,
sedentary, holding out (not forth),
a modernist hero par excellence.

June 16, 2004

Autobiography

Why set down in detail the life of
someone described once, not unfairly,
as 'the man who never was'? How
can you write the biography of one
who devised dozens of names for
pieces of himself when he did not,
would not or could not be himself?
Better to set down your own auto-

biography or, better still, probe the life
of a neighbor, who'll probably not kill
you or thank you if and when he finds
out. Don't bother about the dates—
1888 (T. S. Eliot's and O'Neill's,
too) or 1935—and don't mention his
schooling, all of which, practically,
took place in South Africa, instruction

in English. Don't slip into the destructive
element by mentioning the death of
the father when he was five or six or
his mother's remarriage or the string
of children (some dying soon, others
outliving him) that filled his stepfather's
house in Durban, or that the family
doctor at the time fathered a poet, Roy

Campbell, who would follow our poet in
school (where he saw his predecessor's
name—or initials, I forget which—carved

on his desktop, he claimed). Forget his jobs,
back in Lisbon—boring beyond words—
setting up a print shop-publishing house (quick
failure), amanuensis (at the typewriter) for
various firms in the Baixa, librarianship up

the coast (oops, he didn't get that job; there
was another candidate), and unremunerated
projects, such as inventing a translation
typewriter, a *planta* for Lisbon, etc. etc.
Editing *Orpheu* and *Athena* fill out the list,
glorious now for those who continue to
count on such things. Death at forty-seven
but not before winning a second first prize

(or was it a first-time second prize—nobody
remembers, nor does it matter) and not before
recognition by the swaggering literary boys
in Coimbra. Death at night in the French hospital,
the English hospital but a stone's throw away
from his bedroom—nice touch to a life such as
his, but only filler. The seemingly bottomless
trunk, left behind, that raises an eyebrow but soon

becomes just the fetish, all-enveloping for those
who won't recognize it as such. Posthumous
publication of stuff he stuffed away to bear
witness to a life still unlived—the real story
but hardly the stuff of a biography. Then the
heteronyms, each with things of this world,

but that's another story, not this one. I've
forgotten Ophelia; but so did he—twice.

Apr. 15, 2005

When Orpheus Died

The *Times*, New York's paper of record,
failed to make it news, though when,
in the same year, Itamaraty's Ronald de
Carvalho cracked-up and died, the *Times*
dubbed him the 'king of Brazilian prose.'

May 5, 2005

Authors and Their Papers

In Paris, Hemingway's
suitcase is left behind
(it is said) in a taxi.

The poet's landlord
In Paris confiscates
Sá-Carneiro's trunk.

Himself wills his stuffed
box to his Lisbon family.
It swells and ramifies.

Aug. 3, 2005

Caeiro Speaks

Had I had the misfortune to live my life
in Lisbon, we wouldn't have been friends.

Space and good timing, as it happened,
spared me that embarrassment, that

having to put up with self-compromise,
a stain of accommodation to that city man

de pouca confiança, always on his way
to sit in the fumes of some café or bar.

Oct. 7, 2005

Lines of Attraction

Emerging crane-like from the open maw
of the underground station immediately
fronting *A Brasileira* a few meters short
of the poet's church, now undergoing a

facelift in preparation for great Catholic
things, I see, again, of a Saturday morning
in this busy place, sunny after several days
of what everyone says is sorely needed rain,

tourists queue up to perch besides the man in
the hat, looking to have their pictures taken,

some sure to end up in my pictures, too, lost
there forever or for as long as prints will fade.

Oct. 22, 2005

Discovery

Men of action stand, men of thought sit. So much I
learned when they slipped the canvas from the sitting
Infante Henrique in Fall River in 1939, so much was
confirmed when I first looked up at the Camões of the
Chiado. So then when will the sitting Pessoa, also of
the Chiado, stand up and run, down to the Cais de
Sodré, to the river, the sea?

Nov. 12, 2005

Me and Him

No one sees me do it but once in
a great while I avert my otherwise

steady gaze so as to catch a glimpse
of sea somewhere beyond the Cais

de Sodré. Not so far as he did I sail
but no less frequently and all in my

formative years. He never takes his
eyes off the portion of the city he has

come to know the hard way. Under my
feet is a station of the metro, beneath his,

a car park. There's luck in the draw, I will
say, when it's accomplished posthumously.

Nov. 23, 2005

No Pessoa in Toronto

With a hundred thousand countrymen moving
about in a place that is more like New York
or Chicago than any city in the U.K., there is

still no place or thing, no sprig of history or
thought original enough to inspire in me even
the twinge of an easy or shameless wanderlust.

Nov. 23 / Dec. 17, 2005

M.I.A.

I've looked, I've looked,
and I've looked still again,
but I cannot find the verses
and stories you may have
squirreled away in the U.K.

Leads in letters—to *Cassell's*,
to *Punch*—have led, so far, to

dead ends. Except for *The
Athenaeum* that one time,
did no one see merit enough

to allot you a quarter-page or
to turn to you to fill the three
or four inches left over when
someone else's bit had run
short? Might it have made a

difference to your vita, adding
a few lines to your resume, when
you over-reached yourself for
that little job in Cascais? Did
it change your life, I ask?

Dec. 15, 2005

O poeta é um fingidor

This poet lies a great deal.
He lies in three major languages.
Maybe this poet lies all the time.
His every thought must be a lie.
Catch him once and he dies.

Apr. 4, 2006

Santos da casa

Imperturbable, he
is the constant thing

in the middle of a
crowd as well past

midnight festive
youth stream deep

into *bairro* streets,
rising and failing

in their pretextual
duty to São João.

An old crone sits
fixed in the chair,

her back to the man.
She will not scare.

June 24, 2006

Away from the Coast, in Oeiras

The Parque de Poetas concentrates
its *hommage* in a declension of choice
names writ in bold under living feet.
The modern magi of our *salty*

tongue (as Alberto puts it), some
of them also appear in stone in mini-
parks apart, sculpted in large and
heavier, surely, than life. Yet he is as
he is in the Chiado in the common
photos, though now his shoes, brutish,
cement him in place. Over there, Sá-
Carneiro slumps, and way over there
sylphlike women sprout awkwardly
from David's neatly sliced head.

June 25-26, 2006

Fresh Face

Medals, medallions, and coins
are struck, and so, too, are poses.
Cameras candidly record all this,
for they are integral to the stance
if it is to last beyond the fading
memories of those who've seen
Jerónimo to the Master's left—
o blessed is the photographer!
the utilitarian shutter-bug!

July 21, 2006

Ibis

So there it is,
the key to the secret
so publicly proclaimed
in a business trademark,
so privately practiced

to amuse children,
the stork-like stance,
standing on one leg,
the other leg bent at the knee
so as to cross the other.

I might have known
that it goes all the way
back to the Greeks,
to Callimachus from Cyrene
(*c*. 320—*c*. 240 B.C.E.),

to be exact. It is Ovid's
translation of *The Ibis*
(the original is lost) that's
been described as "a
fearsome pasquinade

about the carcass-eating
stork, a bird 'full of filth'"
—a meaning semiotically

withheld from the innocent
book buyer, if not the child.

Oct. 2, 2006

Off in the Corner

In the old picture of Black Horse
Square, from a vantage of the river,
the right hand corner of the Arcade
is plainly visible but empty of everyone,
as is the rest of the square, unpeopled
as if in a period of historical transition.
To come, of course, are those who would
make of the corner the place that it would
become to this day when even indifferent
food and bad service cannot drive away
those who sniff for signs of *Orpheu*'s
crazies. Except for the arcade's visible
signage, any pre-dawn cell phone picture
transmitted today would look the same.

Oct. 5, 2006

Flotsam, Jetsam

Looking for Mr. Person, John Wain got one name wrong at
        first, calling him Alfredo de Campos, thinking,
        perhaps, of J. Alfred Prufrock.

His American heteronym is what Edwin Honig called himself,
and Edouard Roditi introduced the name and art of
Lisbon's Ibis to Paul Celan, who wrote his name on
water.

José Blanco wrote estimable prose in the voice of the Master,
in Landorish imaginary interviews.

Antonio Ferro's way to a personal hell was paved, Portuguese
style, with good intentions.

Jonathan Griffin's Portuguese was bad enough to free him from
fidelity to the poet's words or ethos.

In 1977 the governor's factotum promised to give him his own
day by proclamation if Mr. Pessoa were to show up in
Providence.

On November 30, 1935, uninvited and unwanted, Death pulled
the final "man from Porlock" moment on the scribbling
man.

James Dickey sour-graped his message that Pessoa's poetry
was not very good, after wanting to emulate him.

Mary McCarthy, who may or may not have read his poetry,
wanted, on the word of the Dutch man with an
agenda, to do in his American translator.

When the Dutch man and the American translator found
themselves in the same hall in Lisbon, they circulated
cautiously so as not to meet face-to-face.

Jerónimo promises to be the newly minted heteronym,
discovering other voices, other persons.

No one knows if he ever read the New York *Times*, which, by
the way, was on sale in at least one venue in Lisbon
in his day.

Why did he never send his poems to the U.S.A.? Was it due
to a disdain for America or simply the high cost of
postage?

Why is there no census of surviving copies of *35 Sonnets*
      or *Antinous* in Scotland, Ireland, or England?
Is Arthur Hugh Clough, a common source, the reason why T.
      S. Eliot's early poetry is so evocative of Pessoa's—
      especially that of Álvaro de Campos?
For the details of the life of Álvaro de Campos look not to
      Clough but to Ernest Dowson (whose poetry also
      anticipates Pessoa's).
Is Clough's *Amours de Voyage* the sustained poem that Álvaro
      tried to emulate but managed to produce only shards—
      like *Poema en linha recta* and *Cruzes na porta da*
      tabacaria?
But what about the great *Tabacaria*, you ask, or the Odes?
      The beat goes on.

Oct. 5, 2006

Aniversário

Never too early to begin to plan
a birthday, and while they lag (so
far as I know), it's not to worry.
120 years, a long time when you're
still alive but not even a blip in
eternity if you've moved on; speak-
ing of moving, where can they trans-
late the bones now? After Prazeres?
after Jerónimos? Durban? Angra
do Heroísmo? the crashing waters
at the Boca do Inferno? I have not
the wit to think of a better place

or the next move. Maybe just a
bevy of books, a spate of conferences,
a new museum, fussing over what
survives of his personal library—
all this is possible if the flesh is
willing, if the proposal is approved,
if the funding is there.

Oct. 19, 2006

3 Takes

Later, an American
poet who was not
Whitman celebrated
himself by pimping:
'Snodgrass is walking
through the universe.'

Ibis didn't know better,
or so we thought,
when he announced
that he was a bit
bigger than that
same Universe.

Mr. tse-tse worried
that his question, an
overwhelming one,
would disturb the

Universe dare he
dare to ask it.

Oct. 23, 2006

A Death Among Poets

> *Morreu Fernando Pessoa. Mal acabei de ler a*
> *noticia no jornal, fechei a porta do consultório*
> *e meti-me pelos montes a cabo. Fui chorar*
> *com os pinheiros e com as fragas a morte do*
> *nosso maior poeta de hoje, que Portugal viu*
> *passar num caixão para a eternidade sem ao*
> *menos perguntar quem era.*
> Miguel Torga, *Diário I*

In his diary, under the date December 3, 1935, three days after Fernando Pessoa's death, these few sentences moved me deeply when I first read them, and they continue to impress me to this day, with the living poet's deftness in turning a diary entry into an uncommonly succinct and moving elegiac record. Calling to account and reprimanding an entire nation for its having forgotten to remember the living poet at the moment of his shockingly early death, Miguel Torga the poet cannot settle for the conventional evocation of nature's mourning of the poet's death by setting down lines of verse, but must set down his humble tribute in a prose account of the way he physically —not in words but in outward action responded at the moment of loss. The physician shut down his practice and walked out into the countryside and to the hills to participate directly— joining the pines and the crags—in nature's own lament for the

114

just fallen poet. Only that extraordinary act itself, not the composition of any formal elegy in the words and images of the study (as some others might have done and later did) would serve to honor the great poet in death. Amen.

Oct. 25, 2006

As Usual

If *a alma do negócio é a propaganda*
(which even I believed when in my cups)
what business, pray tell, does this man
promote, sitting upright on his duff like
that? Is he merely meant to be an updated
memento mori? Or is he there to guide
Christians to their heaven deferred or a
Mussulman to his dreamy reward?

Dec. 17, 2006

A alma do negócio é a propaganda

If you hope to woo the careless horde,
lose the statue, try a sandwich board.

Dec. 19, 2006

The Somatic Lie

Fearing for himself the madness so
evident in his maternal grandmother,
he hit on the notion of using the threat
of imminent derangement to his every-
day benefit. That was the device he
made over to his heteronymic avatar,
who used it to get his coeval out of his
singular sentimental scrape. Adopted,
it was, by others, including Octavio Paz,
who adapted his excuse to the big C,
brooking neither contest nor question.

Dec. 22, 2006

On the Road to Highland

The rest areas on their turnpike
are named to honor Indiana's
famous people, including poets
and other writers. Just their
luck (or his), it must be, that
Pessoa was no hoosier.

Dec. 22, 2006

Mau tempo

Were Caeiro's flocks comprised of *ovelhas* or *carneiros*?
Were some of them more docile than the others?
Were some of Caeiro's thoughts more obstinate than others?
Is sheep-killing weather a form of thought-killing?
Are these merely distinctions without differences?

Dec. 22, 2006

Taine and the Moment

Had he deigned even
once to take the train
to Paris, would the ride
have changed his life
and country's culture?
I don't believe it for a
moment. Now had
Sá-Carneiro stayed put,
that's another matter.

Dec. 23, 2006

Arabica, Robusta

When still a boy Fuentes splashed down
in the bay at Santos on his way to Miami.
Bishop sailed into the same port, as did

Kipling ahead of her. Not one of them
mentions the Santos Coffee Exchange,
though as the port of export, Santos was
once everything to the *fazendeiros do café*,
Paulistas all, *Paulistanos* some. Yet, to
Pessoa, Santos was nothing; no surprise
there, since Brasil itself was nothing more
to him than a place barely suitable as home
to a petulant, cunning, exilic Ricardo Reis.

Jan. 8, 2007

Aguarelas

Standing up in the plane in flight,
he tries on his hat, removes it,
and puts it back in the overhead.
He looks familiar, reminding me
a little of Alfredo Margarido,
whose water-color Pessoas will
outlast his essays, I'm afraid,
or, better still, he recalls
Alexandrino, the plumber, leaning
over the bowl, wrench in hand,
wreaking his miracle of making
water flow and then stopping it.
A chance association, a trivial
connection, a fortuitous find,

but hats off to them both for
believing in civilization.

Jan. 8, 2007

Child Aboard Aircraft

High over somewhere,
a few hundred miles
from Albuquerque,
there pops into my
mind the upshot of
an exchange with
a physicist, who, I
later learned, had
been awarded a gold
medal by the Acoustical
Society of America—
a conversation in which
he informed me that
he had looked it up
found that the word
hyperacusia, according
to his books, was no
word at all.

Ah, but the word—
dictionary-legitimate
or no—was once used
by one poet (Pessoa)
to speak of his and

Edgar Poe's affliction.
How lucky for me, I
who am the first one
to put into print this
spot-on neologism.

Jan. 12, 2007

Beggars Would Ride

Had he lived to his majority in Lisbon, the city of his birth, and
then set out on his travels, to the far reaches of earth, he might
have composed a native poem worthy of his own designs. As
it was, the Durban of his youth—into an exile too soon forced
upon him—was of no worth. Even the language, his second
one, learned well enough to win him the Queen's prize for
expression—or was it exposition?—served mainly to feed his
quixotic dream to be some day counted among the greats of
England. Maybe a travel grant, after his return to his own
native land, one that would take him to London, to Glasgow, to
Dublin, even—ah, but there were no such horses then.

Jan. 12, 2007

Blessing

The young German kneels before his mother.
He is about to go off to war, I surmise. She'll

not see him again, of course, but for now he is
his mother's living, loving, breathing boy.

What wall in what dining-room of what boarding
house did this lithograph adorn? Somewhere in
Lisbon is all we now know, and that because
the poet countered with *O menino da sua mãe*.

Jan. 18, 2007

The Appels

Today the Appel on the floor for the Stanford
University woman's basketball team sparks a
thought. Is it odd that Pessoa should have studied
English and German languages and literature
with one Alfredo Appel in 1905-06 while a second
Appel, also Alfred, and once a professor at Stanford,
should have become expert in all things Nabokov,
culminating in a fulsomely annotated *Lolita*?
A stretch, perhaps, indicative of an unruly mind.

Jan. 17, 2007

Tell Him Something He Doesn't Know

"That's what you do when you're married:
you irritate each other," said a mother to
her daughter as they headed out to the food
court. Fernando never married, having

already more irritation than he could
handle, and, of course, she wasn't *really*
a fiancée. No, she wasn't—not *ever.*
Well, not the second go-round, anyway.

Feb. 10, 2007

On the Road Again

It is the 28th of
February and,
I, like Caeiro,
greet the sun.
Simply that.
Nothing more.

A silver town-car,
a red stripe across
the top of its wind-
shield and a hand-
printed sign reading
MONTIERO [*sic*]
will take me to
Mineola to talk
about poets—
not F.P. this time,
but W.C.W.

There resemblance
ends, for one was
a fulltime physician

married to a Flossie,
the other a homespun
metaphysician who
spurned his Ophelia.
There's no shadow-
boxing the one with-
out hearing the other.

Feb. 28, 2007

The Armatures of Porfirio Lindoso

Wire twisted into figures
of the self-same he
riding a bicycle or standing
by a lamp post—these and others
—selling out of a gimcrack shop
hard by his commemorative
rooms.

Today I see the shop has dropped
the folk in the name of Art.

What wire figures?
Wire figures?
Who?

Feb. 28, 2007

The Gentleman of Shallot

Yeats had his Maud Gonne and Hardy his Emma,
but Ophelia, kind and generous, sweet and young,
it turned out, was no muse, at least not to me.
A skeptic I was, or so I determined, a puritan
to the bone, turned on by the work, metastasis,
allowing no will to revise, no desire to debride.

Mar. 24, 2007

Coleridge

He said it and I believed it—for a time.
"It is the perfection of womanhood
to be characterless. Everyone wishes
a Desdemona or Ophelia for a wife—
creatures who though they may not
always understand you, do always
feel you and feel with you." *Oxalá*.

Mar. 28, 2007

Por lapso

explains his editor, having changed
the original "Borges" to "Soares"—
no more, no less, and, of course, not
enough. Let's say, for the sake of
argument, that Soares, too, had his

own second identity, and that identity
was known to some other, an exploited
office worker, just like Bernardo.

Apr. 17, 2007

My People

Álvaro de Campos traveled about—
not I; Ricardo Reis went into exile for
me; and Alberto Caeiro died for himself.
Bernardo Soares sighed hard and long
for me, and while Charles Robert Anon
dropped out of sight, as did his brother
Alexander (for whom nobody looked),
the Baron Tieve (a Sidney Carton, less
stoic than depressed but never heroic),
took his life for me. As for the others,
let's just say I lost interest. Yet when I,
too, left, some will recall that operatic
Álvaro dropped into bottomless silence,
I'd like to think, in memory of me.

Apr. 22, 2007

One Leg Crossed

In the stiff-dreary effigy
you cannot discern
that the hat band is black,

and as shiny as the black
shoes, a match that pleased
or comforted a low-grade
depressive like me, one
yearning to be comical.

May 3, 2007

Concordance

My God! Six decades after my birth there is still
no possibility of a concordance to my work! O.K.,
so I left the trunk brimming with paper, some of it
organized, some of it seemingly in order, and some
of it, frankly, dropped in at random. If I only had
had the time to bring it all to order, my biblical
span of three score and ten. Oh, who am I fooling?
Who's fooled by this sham of a complaint? By now
everybody knows (as I well knew then) that I was in
the business of making trouble, adding paper to paper,
including the sheets showing forth grandiose plans for
numerous books—plans that my posthumous editors
and compliant publishers have fretted and fussed over
ever since. And of course the critical edition itself
only adds to the problem, creating books and series
of editions when none was intended. Was it all really
work toward, a record of process sans end, an end
that was less an end in sight than a necessary illusion
to keep the ass in blinders from seeing another way—
a way away from the milling task? Just print it all on
paper cut into pages, number the pages and the lines

on the page, and get on with the concordance; after all,
only the words count, only the words are fixed, only
the individual words have the ring of fact or fiction.

May 4, 2007

Campos Sputters

an end to poems about poetry
an end to poems addressing the word
an end to the poet in awe of his own poem and the poem that
        would make more of things than they can bear
and while we're at it, an end to lines like these

May 5, 2007

Babel

I set out to master Portuguese when I learned that in
Lisbon, the city of my birth, no one spoke my language.

May 7, 2007

Polygenesis

When Jacques, through Shakespeare,
gave word to the commonplace thought
that a man in his time plays many parts,
he blazed a trail for a deviant poet, one

that would assign all such parts to peeps
who, slipping their traces, played them.

June 6, 2007

The Odd Fact

> *Quis o acaso que Almada Negreiros falecesse,*
> *a 15 de Julho de 1970, no mesmo quarto*
> *do Hospital de S. Luís onde, em 1935,*
> *morrera Fernando Pessoa (que ele pintou).*
> *Boletim* (Instituto Camões) (1993)

Who discovered this coincidence and how soon? Was it
Armando Côrtes-Rodrigues, who managed to be the last
one of the *Orpheu* crowd to survive Almada? Or was it
Gaspar Simões, always at his job? Almada had his life, as I
had mine, though mine did not match his in public acclaim,
government patronage. Maybe if I had lived longer, Ferro
would have done as much for me as he did for him. Still, the
prize for *Mensagem* was nice, and one must not begrudge
others their boon. So, we two ship out from the same bloody
hospital room and—a miracle—somebody notices.
I could tell you things. Almada could, too.

June 7, 2007

An Unmade Film

Chapeus há muitos, seu palerma!
stars Vasco Santana and Antonio
Silva, the former as Sá-Carneiro,
the latter as you-know-who. Set
in such places as Lisbon, Paris,
Mozambique, in the 1910s, it is
a comedy, of course, sending
the boys to and fro looking for
Mário's father's money to publish
Orpheu ad infinitum (or a third
issue, if it came to the fore).
Farce—very—things like a crowd
chase during which Mário steals a
hat and Fernando stands the ibis.

June 10, 2007

Not on Your Life

The death of Michael Hamburger
does and does not diminish me.
It will not be put thus by anyone
who would eulogize this German
exile—the last of those Englishmen
who first made much of me, lending
an ancient-alliance kick to the cause
of a posthumous life. Quintanilha,

Griffin, Rickard and Wain—a poet
told them who by telling them why.

June 28, 2007

Cliché

Pestilent teaching to full bloom comes when the drive to
correct lays waste the desire to create. Take Harold's notion
that poets "correct" poems by other poets who just didn't see
where they were going, where, in fact, they were going wrong.

Perhaps I, too, behave in such a way that encourages my
readers to believe that my poems are intended to "correct" the
poems of predecessors, that, for instance, *Ela canta, pobre
ceifeira* "corrects" the whole of *Solitary Reaper*, when, in fact,
I wasn't even able to "redirect" the poem. (Try "correcting"
"stout Cortez" to "stout Balboa" in Keats's sonnet and see
where it gets you.)

No, there was no redirection, let alone correction, in *Ceifeira*;
a poem cannot but honor the strong poem that gives it its first
breath, lends it its bone.

June 30, 2007

Back at Ya, Gil Vaz

When I am tired of thinking out paradoxes
or faulty, jerry-built syllogisms or simply

weary of things as they are, I take down your
poem, not to luxuriate before its lines of high
falutin insincerity, released at the flood, but to
fish for feelings alien to these troubled waters.

July 11 / 22, 2007

Casais Monteiro

One of Sena's anxieties was that he wanted to be you,
Margarido once said (to a person whose identity does
not matter at the moment), but wasn't. What a curious,
mean thing to say. No matter. In 2008, surely, the
Jornal de Letras will celebrate your centenary, well-
chosen contributors who will praise your poems, the
poems of the advocate of sincerity (without claiming,
as did Alfredo to the same one whose identity still does
not matter, that you were the great poet of your time,
while Sena was no poet at all), as well as your well-
crafted essays, redolent of your high seriousness. The
piece will remind readers that you were instrumental in
establishing my literary reputation. There will be nothing,
I suspect, about the coincidence that in your latter years
you broke bread with citizens of the United States of
America, a country whose independence day falls on July
fourth, too, a birth date in common but a fact ignored.
There will be something about your long exile in Brazil.
If you are still in character, you'll see it all as another
chance to turn up your nose—vanity of vanities—and
dismiss it: "*Não li, e não gostei.*" (even if the quip did
not originate with you). Why did you not follow my

example? Papers? None to speak of—no forage for nibbling
sheep, for antsy goats. But my stuff—the copy of the book I
inscribe to you—I'm happy to say, sells, on the internet.

Aug. 27, 2007

Made Man

"Pessoa-like," one David Mason says—
just like that—when he wishes to indicate

that the poet Fairchild "expands his aesthetic
range" by "taking in other personae."

Blessed be the translators, who carry him
over into English so that even those with

little or no Portuguese can hoist him to use
—shorthand, reaching ears already in on it.

If the great names of his time did not speak
in tongues, these, unknown to him, do.

Sept. 18/29, 2007

Degrees of Separation

If Roy Campbell is to be trusted—and he can't be (trust me)—
a school boy scratched my name, perhaps more than once,
on the surface of a desktop in Durban. Horrors! Not even

Chevalier de Pas would do that! No, not that entertaining
intimate of my childhood, nor any of the contributors to the
Palrador; after all, any new scratching on the surface of my
desk would be ascribed, of course, to me. Campbell never
knew me, an older boy, and I didn't know him, even though
it is written that his father was doctor to our family. But
Campbell, without recourse to the occult, devised a link, one
plausible, perhaps, to those who don't know me, to Pessoa
and his work. Add to it that he, a South African (as I would
have been considered to be had I stayed in Durban) achieved a
standing in English poetry (now, sadly, greatly diminished—
his situation, not mine) that I, callow youth that I was, could
only aspire to (as I do still) but not achieve. Search and Anon,
means and ways to that end, came into being, too precocious
to last. Roads diverged, and I being many, made the most
of them, dividing and sub-dividing as I went, not always
consolidating, and always failing to bring them to book. Not
even in the last full year of my earthly and bodily life, when
I cobbled together a modernist epic (although I never made
that claim for it) into shape and form (at least spaced out on the
page) than my unknown-to-me Anglo-American competitor
could manage when he, too, strove to shore up his fragments.
His poem he gave to the *Dial* for the magazine's then hefty
prize; mine went to Antonio Ferro and S.N.I. for a piece of the
brand-new Antero de Quental Prize for the best book of poetry.
We were both needy, I guess, though, other things being equal,
I'd venture to say that my need was the greater. Still, our grasp
betrayed our reach and once such a thing is done (between the
thought and the act always falls the shadow—I'll grant him
that), there's no forgiveness (I'll grant him that, too). Yet the
American the Brits allowed to be English saw his poems slip
easily into their literary tradition, alongside the Irish Swift,

Shaw, Yeats, Synge, Wilde and Joyce (here I go, another list),
while mine... Maybe it's just that my time is yet to be, when
the explicit *Antinous*, or the Breughel-like wedding orgy, or
that set of arch and egregious sonnets find backers. But this *is*
an old story, boring me to death, though I'll tell it again, not at
the drop of a hat, but when I catch your eye. Try me.

Nov. 19, 2007

Californias

What need had I to see the great American West when I
had journeyed to the Alentejo, seeing there all I needed
to see of cow country? And need I say anything more
about the earth's answer to the fools searching for gold
in an El Dorado out of time and place? I went to buy a
printing press; in 1848, no it was 1849 ("forty-*niners*,"
remember?) and it was gold ("fool's gold" wastes an
adjective) found at Sutter's Mill, that Marshall bruited
loudly about. A golden goose for a few, it proved to be,
but for most a wild goose chase. Records are spotty; but
if truth be known, there was more gold in the talking than
ever panned out. The Azorean who went for the gold
stayed for cows. But that story's somebody else's affair.

Nov. 20, 2007

Zero Sum

cogito ergo sum (Descartes)
trust the cup, trust the saucer (Carver)

veni, vidi, vici (Caesar)
silence when clapping stops (Simon)

all Cretans are liars (Onésimo)
o poeta é um fingidor (Pessoa)

Dec. 8, 2007

The Return of the Native

An outsider in the far reaches of the Queen's Empire, I
was screwed from the get-go. The prize for proficiency
in the language creamed the jest since by law Oxford
and Cambridge were not for the likes of foreigners,
while my Durban-born half-brother got to live his life
in London, a place foreign forever to me. Harder than
hard it was, I tell you, for a young poet with all his eggs
in English baskets to go native in the Lisbon of his past.

Dec. 10, 2007

In All Familiar Places

In the largest bookstore around the Place Sorbonne
I checked out the numerous shelves devoted to the

Pleiade editions to see if your volume—hefty—is
in its place, only to find it missing, its existence
marked by its empty place—a gap in the sequence.
There's a run on Pessoa, I quip to myself—and then,
more seriously, I think—well, at least somebody else
is interested enough to take your book off the shelf
and off to some other place, if only to peruse a few
pages. Should I try to find the book at FNAC (where
I saw it yesterday), if only for the sake of its notes
and annotations? Surely, none can match Roger
Asselineau's identification in the *Pleiade* Heming-
way of the Fordham Flash, Frankie Frisch, as a
notable religious thinker, which, of course, for all
I know (it occurs to me now) he may have been.
I wonder though what the editor of the *Pleiade*
Pessoa makes of Carrie Nation (if, of course, the
editors ran the spoof on Temperance in America).

Dec. 11, 2007

Literary Taste

Hemingway cannot be translated into Portuguese,
said Elizabeth Bishop, because repetition is anathema

to the Portuguese. Of course I can't tell, since I never
read Hemingway or any other American of the day.

Dec. 28, 2007

Post? Post? Eh What?

Somebody said "post-Salazar, post-Pessoa"
at the Modern Language Meetings in Chicago
this year. Salazar (not to mention Eduardo
Lourenço Faria) bears a certain physical
resemblance to me, although I was a walker
in the city (check the photos) while he rode
about in a car—safer that way, I suppose.
I suppose he and I—I refer to Salazar—shared
some minor ideas about the people. (It was
altogether fitting, I suppose, that Vasco Reis
was the committee's choice, if not Ferro's.)
Still, I object to having my named linked, in
the same sentence, to Salazar's, especially
when the times are not clearly "post" for me
(or my coterie) or, I fear, for him either.

Dec. 28, 2007

Literary Borrowings

I pretty much stopped with the so-called
English Decadents, the poets of the 1890s,
among whom, of course, I number Yeats
with all his Celtic claptrap. The three big
heteronyms come from that cheerily morose
bunch, though I always felt free to select freely
those aspects, attitudes, attributes (to stop
at three) to construct my coterie of betters.
In fact, I built better than I knew, you might

say, since if my life depended on it (again
I might say) I could not say where or from
whom I got anything that matters from my
virtual musketeers. Love for the pubescent
girl in Dowson, lust (repressed) for the boy
in Johnson, and so forth. You get the picture.
Yeats? He gave me nothing. I'm told his
work improved later on. I'm skeptical.
But I hope so, for the sake of his readers
(who could never have amounted to many).

Dec. 28, 2007

You Speak of Carrie Nation

Portugal never had a Carrie Nation, not ever.
Imagine chopping up a tavern, putting *galegos*
out of work, annoying their crows, disturbing
ravens. Bright's disease? Cirrhosis? A trade-
off, I tell you, straight up, a no-brainer.

Dec. 28, 2007

Seas Never Sailed

Had I sailed west I could have become an American at
seventeen, just as Eliot became English, and O'Neill a
dramatist. I'd have done alright. But think of the annals
of Portuguese poetry had I become the Henry Green of
Portugal, though who would have noticed?   Scholars would

have knocked me into the Whitman tradition or the Poe camp
—me, a near-contemporary of Wallace Stevens, Hart Crane,
and the Jewish, English, Hispanic heteronym-in-the-mirror
who never recognized the makings or the markings.

Dec. 28, 2007

Pano pra manga

Who can say what the family knew?
All I know is that they kept the box.

Feb. 10, 2008

Lena Grove Lives

At the Espresso Bar in Avery Fisher Hall
(home of the New York Philharmonic), I
buy a cup of coffee at a price that would
throw the Minotaur off his feed. Off to

the side, a young Amerasian singer finishes
off his interview conducted by another Asian.
Yesterday he had a birthday—not the singer
or the interviewer. One hundred nineteen,

a long run, and it grows longer by the year.
How good to see him on the alternate pages
of my first-ever Portuguese passport, sharing
billing with his coeval for the ages. Camões

would be surprised, I think, to see so many
Asians in this part of the New World, at the
Lincoln Center, having himself co-habited
with many of them *in situ*. The poet failed

to double the cape, never beheld the Indias
or the coasts of China or Japan. In the mine-
fields of the imagination this fact seems not
to have mattered, well, only to the Almirante.

Feb. 14, 2008

Lunch Poem

"Surely he thought better of it,"
they'll say. They will be wrong.
I never thought better of anything
or anyone. The words moved.

Mar. 7, 2008

A Passing

The teapot is broken. . .
not the choicest piece
in the cupboard, but
always functional, and
for a time constantly in
service; others were brilliant,
showy, living up to fashion,

to popularity, yet none was
ever busier.

Mar. 13, 2008

Cognition

Up close nothing works as
well as it does at a distance.

Mar. 20, 2008

Parallel Canon

As I said to Mario Beirão on 1 Feb. 1913,
ideas and projects and whole poems swirled
through my consciousness, moving too fast
to be domesticated by words set down on
paper. A whole literature—lost for good.
No boast. No regrets. No tears.

Mar. 27, 2008

So That Was It

Only now, after these many years
of my posthumous existence, have

I tumbled to the fact that the Porlock
interruption in Álvaro's sonnet about

his heart, so heartfelt in the bud, was
his metaphor of an admiral, and not

just any old admiral but Gama himself.
I wondered, at the time, why he offered

me the sonnet for my *Mensagem* but
daft though I be myself, I never for a

moment considered the offer of his daffy
sailor, doomed to longing for the sea.

I didn't have the temerity (or heart) to tell
him his poem was poor poetry and, to boot,

bad history too. He longed to lodge his old
boy somewhere. But not in my house!

Apr. 5, 2008

Tomorrow

Toe-tags in a morgue those numbers assigned
to each piece of paper in the *baú*, it's enough
to make a body cry; the simulacrum of order,
sequence, epistemic, purposeful, conclusive,

mimicking all those promising syllogisms
fading away before delivering, as promised.

Apr. 14, 2008

Ricardo Reis's Query

After the years and the words,
how could he not have recognized
that Álvaro's admiral, condemned
to a landlubber's asylum, hostage
to the memorial habits of muscles
and marrow, had a history?

Apr. 26, 2008

Dead Serious

Let's get down to making some so-so invidious comparisons.
Shakespeare was a businessman, a property owner, a stage
and theatre manager, I was none of these, though I tried to be
an inventor, a printer-publisher, a librarian, and failed, period.
He had the Globe for his stage, I had none, losing the Teatro
San Carlos at my doorstep when I was six without ever having
been inside. He courted favor among his betters and got it, I
courted favor among my peers—what a self-aggrandizing lot
we were—and found it got me nowhere worth going. He left
no papers but a will, I never got around to a will, thinking, of
course, that I had plenty of time to draw one up. Besides what
legacy was there? Some books, my eyeglasses, a hat, umbrella,

a pen? Even the trunk was nothing more than just a receptacle to box my scraps, my plans, my letters out of sight, away from the eyes of those women who kept up my room. Order on the outside; chaos within. How much time and effort wasted when I had to ferret around in the papers, dig down into the mass to find something I thought was there! If he had a trunk of papers it was never found or, better still for his posthumous fame, emptied out, papers scattered or burned. Enough of this talk about scraps and shards, stolen and lost, not extant for never having existed in the first place. Here's an odd fact. When I died in 1935 I could say I had put into print more of my writings than he had in 1636. Good thing for him he had those friends and foes, acquaintances who (literally) remembered his plays and found printers avid enough to see profit in the venture. I had a few of them, too, those who started me at Ática.

Apr. 28, 2008

Improving the Night

Each night in my room at Rua Coelho da Rocha, no. 16, 1º Dtº
when I was not too drunk to see, I would lift the lid of the box,
remove some papers, place them around the room, and find,
each time, a new order for my thoughts. As time went by,
however, there were more and more recent papers to get
through so that, time always being short, I found myself
moving ever more slowly. I fell further and further behind.
I took to bringing out scraps and sheets by the handful,
stacking them along the walls, and then starting out anew
in an old place among the shards. The upshot, of course,

is that things got swapped around each time I put them back
in the box. They all knew what I was up to, but no one ever
disturbed me in my room evenings or night. Of course, there
were times, too, when my petty rage for order gave way to
the pleasure of renewing the mounting hoard of papers.

May 3, 2008

Dorothy's Unwritten Poem

Neither one of us, to tell the truth, had enough
sympathy (or sympathy of the right kind) to get
it right. The solitary reaper was not alone (or at
least not lonely). She had her song, which was
part of her as much as it was part of the universe.
She was her song while paying tribute to the
world's work. Not even Stevens got that right,
though he came closer to the strain than did
Wordsworth (or I, who couldn't carry a tune).

May 7, 2008

Raid

An American translator of my poems into English
balked at the word "raid" (employed in the guidebook
found among my belongings) to mean "landed," as in,
that Brazilian aviator in 1922 or so (along with every-
body else, I thought I'd never forget his name) made
his "raids" seemingly at will. The word emanated from

newspapers and photo-rich magazines, of course. So
few of us had any experience whatever with any sort
of aero plane or airship. In any case, deciding that
the word was misused, an instance of poor English,
and saying so in print, the American incurred the wrath
of the *pessoana* preternaturally blue-eyed by virtue of
contacts. Possibly both of them went wrong, each in
a unique way. Let me just put that into play. Santos
Dumont, that's it, the very name comes now to mind.

June 10, 2008

No Ifs, No Buts

To be adept at a myriad of genres
seems to have diminished my chances
at the great prizes. To be a poet of
indifferent lines and a casual essayist
(a local example) hurts not at all the
case for the accomplished novelist.
So he gets a Nobel. The Irish poet
boorishly insists on his plays and
other divagations but it is his remaking
-of-himself in poetry that takes him
to the top. Thus the American person-
of-almost-all letters will never make it,
just as neither would I have made it,
even had I lived long enough to make
a decent run at it. That's where Sena

comes in, in the company of those bad
angels who scattered words to the winds.

June 11, 2008

Parallel Lines

In California (San Ramon to be more exactly local) I
hear a lecture on puppetry and the dramatist O'Neill,
who, as coincidence has it, was by four months my
junior, both of us born behind the eights, so to speak.
My thoughts go out, after these many years of leveling,
to his honors and rewards, the many Pulitzers, a Nobel,
looming high against my shared Antero de Quental.
No matter. As I say, the great leveler. Back to puppets,
though, those marionettes, to be more precise, who were
made to perform O'Neill's plays. Only that artist far
from Lisbon who could have sat me down—Fernando—
on the lap of a generic heteronym, would have caught
me red-handed, acting out my *folie*. Still, such a talk
on the very anniversary day of my birth—and dedicated
to me!—would take my breath away (so to speak).

June 14, 2008

Cicero

Saramago got it right, mainly,
my return to Lisbon after his
death, the shacking-up with

the maid, and all that stuff.
What he didn't know, though,
was that I returned from America,
all right, but not from Brazil.
Chicago was my home town
(actually Cicero), a land of
life lived, not that far from the
city where I earned my living
as a medico—not to the rabble,
canalha, or the mob—but to
the Family itself and its Capo.
His death—not the Capo's,
the poet's—brought me back.
No, alas, that was not the way
it was, not at all, Lídia, for
as you above all others know,
I would never have seen any
point in taking action, knowing
it would not matter not just
at the end but at the moment
of its doing. Dust to dust, even
among the first American Romans...
You know the rest of my affect-
less tune. Sorry, though, about
the affair with the maid, the turn
of the screw in Saramago's bold
and prurient pipe dream.

July 16 / 18, 2008

Cold Case

In every dismissal there is homage.
I don't believe that it is entirely true,
but it is still a good rule of thumb.
Take the reviewer at the *Times* (not
London's but New York's) who writes
that "if Seamus Heaney's *oeuvre* [yes,
he says *oeuvre*] was revealed to have
been written by a Portuguese guy living
in Toronto… it would disrupt our entire
sense" of his poetry. Explain, please.

July 21, 2008

The Knock

There was never a man of Porlock
in my life, at least not after I moved
in with my aunt and, later, my sister,
gate-keepers insuring not so much
my peace and quiet as fostering the
dismal science of family, to disrupt
my train of thought. Whatever I left
unfinished I left unfinished because
I distracted myself and could not
think, lost soul, how to pick up a
loose thread—bounty to the reader.

Aug. 18, 2008

Kidding the Kidder

It takes two languages to make
this homonym. So pronounce it
how you will it conveys meaning
that encompasses the one the other.
Sá-Carneiro would have loved it,
jokester that he was, to the last.
Nor was Antonio Ferro exempt,
with the game afoot, for he, too,
met Álvaro (but never Caeiro),
somewhere north of Lisbon, far
beyond the Boca do Inferno, the
scene of the biggest joke of all,
though, if truth be known, it, too,
fell finally all too flat. *Merde*.
The joke calls for the suicide
realized, not the deed of a copy-
cat magus in small foreign waters.
What was not a joke was Antonio
Botto's marriage, which freed him
to roam outdoors, undaunted and
unscathed. Ofélia, scathed, un-
aided, played her joke on herself,
played her joke on me and mine.

Oct. 1 / 3, 2008

Panelists

As Elizabeth Bishop said, there's too much green here, green,
      green, green.
But this is not about nature, the natural world, since it is a
      disease of human nature that I reference here.
The needy want to sit or stand to talk and talk at one another
      is what I'm talking about, when envy gets its revenge
      for having envied even envy itself.
Footnote: for the over-greening of Brasil, see Sir Richard
      Burton—not Pessoa.

Oct. 22, 2008

Documentation

If asked, I'd have said
that there were no photos
taken, save a handful in
the company of others,
for the sake of whom
I happened to be there.
Mas os tempos mudam
such that now no one
dare crop me, take me
out of the picture.

Oct. 24, 2008

Statuary

We were drudges, he and I, killing our time in the Baixa,
he ducking in and out of business firms (and just as many bars)
and I most of the daylight hours pecking away at the accounts
of a single firm.
He would not have lasted at what I do and I know that the
quick starts and abrupt ruptures of his days would surely have
ruined me, with my fixed regimen of health and regularity.
With death—his reported in the papers, mine not—we became
none together (and in that one), only, curiously, in time, to go
once again our separate ways.
No matter that we wrote and thought so much alike.
He had his demons, I had mine, and, as the wag has it, never
the twain shall meet.

Oct. 26, 2008

Stations

The visiting poet was handed a sugar packet as a keepsake,
but, always thinking, he scooped up the receipt in the small
dish. On this warm Saturday night in late October *A Brasileira*
swarms with humankind at outside tables (a dog or two taunted
along the way—hint of Breughel). The Poet insists on his
space, never giving up his seat to the milling brood. I would
advise them, were I not such an *acanhado,* to try the heavy
doors to the church across the way, or, better still, drop down

to the Largo de São Carlos, breathe in the starry skies, the well-lit, sharply etched village bell, its middle-of-the-night display.

Oct. 26, 2008

Igreja dos Martires

its bell tower
seen at night
from the Largo
de São Carlos
a beacon for
those in search
of drink, talk,
seduction

Oct. 26, 2008

Amerika

So that's the fabled Brooklyn Bridge seen
in its daily reality from a serviceable train

running on tracks laid over the East River
before plunging into the tunnel light. Hart

Crane questioned why he always saw Poe
emerging from the down-under—a Freudian

sighting if ever there was one. An orphan,
adopted unluckily, this American haunts me

still for his fear made visible by metaphor,
ever facing-off against the common doom.

Nov. 8, 2008

Lorca, Too

In New York, Garcia Lorca saw the unconscious made
visible but neglected to bring his fragments to coherence.
No, he did not, as Frost would say, bring his experience
to book—or, for that matter, to drama, as he did later,
visiting the worlds of Yerma and Bernarda Alba. Or was
it that he ran out of time, too slow to outrun a fascist bullet?

Nov. 9, 2008

Equal Among Equals

Before there was Dowson, of course,
there was Lewis Carroll and his bevy
of Alices, and John Ruskin with his
child bride, or Poe, who theorized his
pedophilia into an aesthetic theory. I
trace my lineage through to these and
all those others unknown to memory,
to recorded history. Doomed, they were,

just like me, to the pleasures of the short-
term, to the fêting of the nymphet.

Dec. 10, 2008

Confession

I wished to be everybody,
to occupy every body, to
think the thoughts of all
—and then to reject every-
thing, bodies, thoughts,
being—to stand alone—
an Alexander, with not a
thing left to oppose me.

Dec. 10, 2008

King's College

Towards the top of the tall,
open-curtained window, a
workman walks the scaffold,
while within they talk of Pessoa.
On the screen sits, discretely, a
legend, but the lamp has reached
the end of its usable life. Please
replace the lamp. No one moves.

Dec. 11, 2008

The List

Hair black as jet dyed to please him still, this
distiller of the dreams of others builds his own
structure of achievement, culminating his un-
wearying task by working through his list of
path-breakers, nine dead and gone, a tenth on
his way but not yet gone. The eleventh is the
un-self-proclaimed *mostrengo* in the room.

Dec. 12, 2008

Not Santa

'Tis the night before and
I'm no Papai Noel, not a
creature is stirring, not
even Álvaro de Campos.
I'm making a list only I
can fulfill. And here is a
mouse (call her Ophelia).
The cupboard is bare
though lined with notes
and scrawls you have to
stand like an ibis to read
at all. To my widows
I bequeath the laundry
lists I never made, to
the men scraps to peruse
and parade. The list is
long and I am short...

But I repeat myself,
I repeat myself.

Dec. 25, 2008

Six Degrees of Ponzi

Apparently Kevin Bacon invested with Madoff
and like everyone else who invested with Madoff,
wittingly or innocently dragging their bundle in
through confidence, lost it all. He—Kevin—
must certainly go all the way back to Sir Francis
Bacon, the jurist-scientist-writer, who took gifts
even as he judged cases (always disinterestedly, it
is said). I shall cast a horoscope—Kevin's—to go
with Francis's. Money, too, speaks in many voices.

Dec. 31, 2008

Good to the Last Drop

Dickinson, before he lived,
asked the only question,
"Does it breathe?"
She too left fragments
that generations embrace,
Maxwell's claim exactly.

Jan. 11, 2009

Lament

At the end I died, he disappeared.
No one there to fluff the pillows.
No little Nell scene for him, not a
distinguished Jamesian moment;
only the *cangaleiro*, humming to
his own muffled drummer. Where
was his cortege? his grieving selves?
Not a hint of Snow White in sight.
Oh, to have been cheated so, after
living out his sorry life in Samarra!

Jan. 14, 2009

Staying the Course

I notice that Horace is always thanking
some God for not having dropped a limb
on his head and that reminds me that I
too am filled with fear when walking in
Lisbon, though trees and limbs are scarce
enough in the metropolis. When the wind
sweeps through the trees in the park holding
Eça hostage, bending branches and turning
leaves over to gray, I find my way elsewhere.

Jan. 14, 2009

Partilhas

So once more it's come to that.
They're selling off the scraps,
those ratty journals left in corners,
most of which I was planning
to sell off pretty much at weight.
And if that's not bad enough,
they're squabbling with young
scholars over transgressions,
imagined and perceived. Let them
have their money, and let the boys
have their copies. A tempest-in-a-
teapot can only—to change the
metaphor—stir the pot, which
needs no stir, no pinch of salt.

Jan. 24, 2009

Nature or Nurture

I had opinions, took stands, and when the polemic
peaked, I intervened, but I didn't have it. The horse-
men had it—especially Caeiro, who had it in spades.
But I lacked it, that panache or swagger or just plain
old confidence. I stood by and they spoke their minds.
How I envied Hamlet, who had attitude enough for all.

Jan. 28, 2009

Overheard

You must not walk by the library without
thinking of him, he who was your bawdy
friend before they welcomed you at the
university, to which place you go this
morning to hear talks celebrating Edgar
Poe on the occasion of the 200th anniversary
of his birth in Boston, Massachusetts.
You do not come as much to the library now,
having been weaned away from seeking the
originals after the dismissal of your *cunha*.
That's not to say that the *Faculdade* does
not have its compensations, the Almada
sketches on the wall to the right of its doors
—a stroke it was, to my liking, that putting my
personae off to the side that way, luring the eye
right at the entrance to the high-walled, waste-
ful, unwelcoming, unventilated, though busily-
enough fenestrated vestibule of this Bauhaus
influenced example of ready-made modernity.
Pity, too, that Pedro's departure has left you
to your own thin and meager devices for gossip.

Mar. 13, 2009

Querying the Critic

Why look out to the east for the mad king of Bavaria, I ask,
when so closer to home I had the young fanatic, encouraged
by Trojan gifts of keepsake, tokens binding him to his name-

sake saint by an admiring papal court? By what excess will
exotic madness exceed the purest of the local products?

Apr. 3, 2009

How It Strikes the Visitor

When the peripatetic Dane, Hans Christian,
set down his tourist's observations after a
visit to Portugal in 1866, he regretted not
having dropped by the great Lisbon cemetery,
Prazeres, but that lapse did not preclude his
thinking that in so calling the place that some-
one or other was demonstrating his sense of
humor, his funny side, one may say, signaled
as well, in *Necessidades*—a queen's palace.

Apr. 22, 2009

Homo laborans

All those tools carefully strewn about the place,
on the landings and in the corners of the stairwell,
even in one instance smack dab in the center of a
room, must have belonged to my brother-in-law.
They were not mine. In fact I never laid eyes on
them. The quickest way to get me to hit the pave-
ment mornings was to remind me that there work-
men coming to fix the pipes. Such work was of
no interest to me whatsoever. It should have come

as no surprise, then, that the typesetters hired for
Olisipo were bound to do me in. I should've seen
it coming even as I negotiated for the contraption
in Portalegre. Marinetti loved the machine, and I
loved the machine. Neither of us liked the mechanic.
Even Álvaro didn't know a ping hammer from a
screwdriver, and he so adept at turning the screw.

Apr. 29, 2009

The Best Elegies

—maybe the only elegies—are not written
out of pain or a deep feeling of the grieving
kind, but about the never known (best), the
barely known (second best) or by commission.
There was a reason for hiring mourners, who,
hands down, drove out the real coin from the
showings that only incidentally call for quid
pro quo. How very like you to mistake over
and over again the genuine feeling for art
that closes the deal, masters the quotation.

May 4, 2009

Ilda Stichini

It was in 1938 that the great Stichini
cast pearls of poetry before the denizens
of New England's Portuguese enclaves.

Camões, Antero, the people's *quadras*
were featured, but she also included me.
Sticking her neck out, but only up to a point,
she offered *O menino da sua mãe* as an
example of "modernism"—surely not for
its irony, I venture. But beggars can't be
choosy; it was a start. It didn't stick.

May 11, 2009

Ex nihilo

Write I always did, whether or not I knew where to begin,
because I always knew I would have something to say. It was
always like that, I like to believe, but maybe it started when
sitting back in my chair at somebody or other's office in the
Baixa, having answered the last London letter, I found I had a
few moments on my hands before moving on to the next firm's
letters. So I wrote, anything at all, and of course it came to me:
my subjects, my verse, my theorizing. Scraps of paper, scraps
of my mind. In the café, of course, it was different. And so,
too, it was at night, standing up to write at my armoire,
especially that night when Alberto spoke and would not stop.
Shepherds, they say, invented mathematics and astronomy
while watching their flocks throughout the night. A congenial
arrangement, I say, one especially suitable for the non-
mystical mystical poet that was Caeiro, my Master.

May 16, 2009

Cadáver andiante

Precocious cadaver, fit for propagating. Indeed.
What a notion. Hardly worth anybody's attention.
Certainly not yours. Still, it was a way of putting
the body in its place and keeping it there. If Mailer
said, when viewing the shelves housing the boxes
housing his words—and he did—that's where we
all wind up, in a box, then the lesser Mailer he.
That sentence shows only that he had little faith
in his own words to keep on fucking—did you
think I didn't know the word? The deed?

May 18, 2009

Dangling Conversation

If all conversations are unfinished at the last,
since death, with no excuse, will drop by,
stopping the mouth as a sort of collateral damage,
this cannot be said of one's readers and critics,
who, always behind in the exchange, will continue
to talk, taking silence for assent or denial as might
be the call at the moment. Of course, this too is an
unfinished conversation thriving on its one-sidedness.

June 24, 2009

164

Barter

What a boon it would have been had I
thought of bartering reading for books,
Nemésio's deal with Bertrand, in which
he got not cash but books of his choice
in exchange for his judgment on sub-
missions. Duck's soup, I say. Instead
I shelled out hard cash—always. Of
course, my reading of English journals
and novels would not have been covered
in such a deal. But who am I fooling.
I'm sure that those many others around
me—all with respectable publishing
(not my case)—never struck such a deal.
My mind wanders. Maybe on the basis
of *my* reports—"Trash! Embarrassing!"
—Bertrand would have published me,
that is, if I could have brought even one
of my pie-in-the-sky projects to book.
But, again, I fool myself, I, who couldn't
even write jokes for the vulgar reader who
plunks down cash for the *Almanaque*.
My big joke, it will be remembered—
twitting my friend in Paris with fake
poems by a spurious poet—backfired
when Sá-Carneiro took French leave.

July 21, 2009

Not Chaucer, Not Vasco Reis

Standing next to—no, walking next to this figure whose face
is hidden in a hooded sweatshirt, I see that we are pretty much
moving together but not ahead, for we walk in place. We do
not get anywhere, though we are stepping forward, aiming to
reach ourselves (or making progress toward the selves we want
to be). How unlike the huddled pilgrims who walked their way
to be there (at least they thought so) at the essence of sanctity,
thinking, I suppose, that some of it would rub off. Yet this is
my kind of pilgrimage. How stupid to think that I could get
somewhere by walking, that people get places by moving their
feet! After all, willy-nilly, I was going somewhere all the time,
in the Chiado or the Baixa, to Abel's or the *galego*'s place
 (where I tried to work up the nosy crows), or even at the high
chest where I set the various boys to play. He who says a
treadmill takes you nowhere talks through his hat or lies.

Aug. 30, 2009

But Who's Counting?

I shall stop setting down these trifles
when the number reaches 200, giving

the whole shebang a purpose neither
deserved nor, truth be told, desired.

Sept.1, 2009

No to the Chelsea

The move cost him nothing, it would seem.
They, his New York publishers, put him up
at the Chelsea, he said, but the not-yet Nobel
rebelled, unwilling, he explained, to put up with
squalor, dirt, vermin, and garbage. He left in
a huff and checked into a nicer berth uptown.
So the cultural histories won't know to list him
among the luminary tenants, before and after
achieving their fame, who hit the sack in this
fabled dump. You know their names, so I won't
rehearse them here, but to the list I add now—
not quite sure that he wouldn't mind it even now
—Saramago's. All I got from America were the
food and exercise fads of McFadden; Campos it
was who discovered Whitman, and, oh yes, there
was Edgar Poe... Odd, though, even I, who knew
better, fancied for myself, in the far-off future,
that showy explosion, that capstone of umbrage.

Sept. 20, 2009

It is Said that Poe Never Laughed

and neither did I, at least not the I who was
always found wanting in everything caught
on Lisbon's screen. But I learned to lay it off
like a bet—the laughter, I mean—on them, my
others, though they were never accommodating.
They said my problem was hysteria—and now

that I think about it—it was Poe's problem, too.
Absurd and silly. But no laughter. Maybe it's
that nothing I say is so, least of all what I say
about myself. Maybe it's that I have forgotten.
Surely Poe laughed, though it didn't make it into
his lines about what it was like when the adults
celebrated his birthday and nobody was dead.

Sept. 30 / Oct. 12, 2009

Álvaro's Not in the Picture

If you don't believe me, look again. No one makes much,
if anything, of that photograph of me with members of my
family, my young niece sitting upright on my lap. Let me
say a thing or two. For starters, notice that she is younger
than Ophelia. Understand? Two, she looks a little startled,
and I'll tell you something else: she never again looked me
straight in the eye after that sitting. Or was it that I never
looked her in the eye? Three—well, there's no three.

Nov. 7, 2009

Pop Quiz for Critics

What thoughts crossed Pessoa's mind as he stood at a urinal?
Did Pessoa think the road to Sintra would take Campos to the
        ends of the earth?
If Caeiro and Elizabeth Bishop were to take one another
        seriously, which one of them would cease to poetize?

Why did Ricardo Reis fall silent when he met Manuel Bandeira
      in the streets of Rio de Janeiro?
If Sá-Carneiro died so that Pessoa could live (as somebody has
      said), who came to life when Pessoa died?

Dec. 31, 2009

Further Discussion

What if Ariadne had miscalculated how much string it would
      take (and thus ran short) to get Theseus to the egress?
If Bishop (Elizabeth) had been struck blind at some point in
      her early days in Brazil, would she have complained
      that there were too many waterfalls?
Would it have made a difference, after all, if Keats answered
      the call as Nightingale?
Was it customary for Saul to bellow as he once did at the
      Brown Faculty Club?
Was it commonality of all the given names in the James family
      that nudged the novelist into allegory—Archer,
      Marcher, Strether, Assingham (first name Fanny)?
How does a potted answer differ from potted meat or a potted
      plant?
What if Emily Dickinson's real friend turned out to be her
      menses, not some cleric in California or Cambridge, or
      an editor in Springfield?
If the islands in the Azorean archipelago had been named for
      the days of the week, which two would have shared a
      name—a different one, in each case?
"Loose lips sink ships" was not an imprecation to write things
      down.

"When we last left..." was how radio stories were revealed to
    be continuations from day-to-day, What, by the way,
    did these folks do on weekends?
Is Bishop's *Fish* ["drink like a fish"?] still another of her so-
    called "alcohol" poems?
Why do the Brazilians so often resort to using the suffix *est*
    in everyday speech?
Everybody has an opinion of Burton's translations of Camões;
    but nobody has read them. Well, not everybody.
When Fernando denied Ofélia for the second and last time, his
    plea was that he reached the decision that he must live
    only for his "work." Convincing?
Pessoa says that no more than six poems end up being all the
    poems for which even the most famous poets end up
    being remembered. What are Pessoa's six? Are there
    six?
He searched for consilience, though neither Pessoa nor anyone
    else at the time, it seems, had the word. Of course, the
    concept is ancient, the proof believed to be everlasting,
    if far from conclusive.

Dec. 31, 2009

2010—2016

Boxing

> *As artes que utilizam o homem como*
> *material vão desda a lucta e o box,*
> *atravez da dança e da mimica, até á*
> *guerra e á politica.*
> Álvaro de Campos (ca. 1924)

> *Terça-feira ultima, realisou-se no*
> *Salão Cinema desta vila [noPico]*
> *uma partida-treino de box entre o*
> *profissional Sr. Alvaro de Campos e o*
> *amador Sr. Manuel Azevedo Lima, sendo*
> *ambos os contendores muito aplaudidos*
> *pela numerosa assistencia. O Sr. Campos*
> *apresentou tambem diversos trabalhos*
> *de ginastica, que agradaram bastante.*
> *Diario de Noticias* (July 24, 1930)

Well, well, *sete pipas e um tunel.*
This will take some looking into!
He told me that all he did there
was cruise the bars and the streets.

Jan. 16, 2010

Riding a Metaphor

What is the opposite of shards, which, after all,
are just pieces broken off some sort of whole
showing, nevertheless, some traces of DNA?
So from any one piece an archeologist should
be able to discern the whole and image it forth
for all to see. This can be done by a team of
apparatchiks. So, too, might the shards of my
baú be arranged to body forth my mind, by way
of model, as I could never have known it. Ah,
but pieces in this case are more like bits of color,
seen beautifully in a kaleidoscope one time and
only once, always to be turned over, ever so
slightly, into another pattern, just as beautiful
and just as unique. After all, I needn't tell you,
a mind is not a pot, nor, shattered, its pieces
shards. You can no more have a unifying theory
(that will hold for more than an instant) than
you can rest at will. Stop for a sip of water, not
to quench a thirst, but to celebrate in satisfaction,
and the kaleidoscope shifts ever so slightly and
its dance of color and light once again becomes
something, of temporary permanence. That's
how I approached what I saw, what I felt, what
I thought. It's but a seahorse, and that's about it.

Feb. 13, 2010

Heavy Lifting

There was no heavy lifting but a lot of walking, as
I made my rounds, not like observing the stations of
the cross, of course, though there were those who
said later that I had martyred myself to scut work
well beneath me, a poet, a thinker, a beau ideal
(to some), in order to pay for my keep. Of course,
my rounds, punctuated by clockwork stops at
watering holes—Abel's, the *Martinho*, the *galego*'s—
kept me frisky, kept me loose. Composing all those
letters in English or French was good practice at
throwing my voice, and my bosses trusted me,
happy to pay me by assignment, never having to
pay me a salary (or the annual Christmas bonus
of a month's wages) and having it understood that
a paid August vacation was out of the question.

Apr. 12, 2010

Once and Future Ghost

Not defended at Harvard, unlisted by the Michigan people
who card such things, not quoted except in lists of the books
left in my library that keep showing up as scholarly references
(a doomsday record, sometimes, of titles now misplaced, lost
or "given a new home"), this text lends substance to shadow.

June 13, 2010

174

So It Has Come at Last—the Distinguished Thing

No one has ever said anything sillier than these,
Henry James's late words. At the end, Saramago
stopped speaking, letting his smile perforce do his
talking, the man of a million words and more, with
so many stories still to tell, surrounded now by his
family, living out his end—not in a hospital bed, as
Sena said all of us must do now-a-days, but more
like Browning's bishop, who dare not stop talking,
pleading for his tomb, fearful for his ducats and the
fate of his jewels, greedy to the last with the sands
of existence sifting slowly through extended hands.

July 10, 2010

Aparencias não iludem

To me he will never be entirely the robust figure that
shows forth in the photographs, for on the one occasion
when I was with him over two or three days, he was
slim and dry, bony and wrung-out, talking about Pessoa
as, predictably, the avatar of the concocted courier the
British salted in the sea off Spain to mislead the Nazis.
This emaciated, old-before-his-time poet, already sick
with the sickness that would in less than a year put him
in his grave, is the one who (to me) wrote all the poems,
all the stories, the criticism, and (my God!) all the letters.
The man in his last year—gaunt, hollow-cheeked, wearing
the tam that had by then become a bit too-big-for-him—is
to me the one who dated his manuscripts and drafts (but of

course there were no drafts). Here was the essential man, parboiled and, more, still simmering. See him in the photo with Gaspar Simões, generals talking war, rumors of war.

Aug. 19, 2010

Ships

In the famous picture where he is famously walking, he faces forward, as if looking at the viewer 80–90 years later. He has just passed a boy, walking away from him on the street-side of the street. Or has the boy just passed him, walking as he is doing on the shop-front side of the walk? No matter, for the boy is not my father (the similarity of their caps has deceived me). Maybe the boy became famous later and the all-unknowing adult has missed his chance to exchange a word with someone who will be great. As for the boy, if he could be thinking about it at all, he is o.k. with things as they go, with ignoring this grown-up, adrift in his wake, forever and a day. Of course, I can crop the boy right out of the picture or, for that matter, crop out, for all time, the suit, hat.

Dec. 2, 2010

Should I Know?

Imitation, the
sincerest form

of —well—
imitation.

Dec. 2, 2010

Natal

Isn't it odd that Jesus is no Saint.
I guess it's like becoming Pope with-
out ever having been a Cardinal or,
better, taking on mortality after having
been born God. There are assumptions
here that I can't get my head around.
I'm not sure about these capitals either.

Dec. 22, 2010

The Status Quo Discomforts

Like Nature, Pessoa wears the colors of the spirit.
I didn't say that. Emerson did—or something like
it, except, of course, it wasn't that exactly. But if
you are particular about the moment and, into the
bargain, particularly careful, Pessoa is your man,
more or less, for all seasons. The lads who circled
him never questioned him (well, not that often),
and that, of course, was the way they liked it.

May 8, 2011

Hit the Duck

Missed the Chicken, and Hit the Duck,
my bemused friend Dave, who had spent
a day or two at Coney Island, I presumed,
was wont to say when the greater reward
resulted from a failure. Apply it to Pessoa,
I say, one who died intestate (at least I did
not see a will the last time I looked into the
Fotobiografia) but with heirs enough to play
fast and loose with access, with permissions,
with royalties. But the foragers came early,
stayed late, and now number into… well,
who knows how many? Even when the cry
went out—*tanto Pessoa já enjoa*—there
was no slack in the cottage—no, mega—
industry. Well Pessoa courted fame for any
and all of his one and many stalking horses.

May 15, 2011

Fact

Romaria by Vasco Reis sells
(on May 17, 2011) for € 200,
Livraria Ferreira, *alfarabista*,
Porto. So it's true: a rising
tide will lift all boats.

May 18, 2011

The American Heteronym

It had to have puzzled his caretakers
to see the burn of his ears just at the
minute he died, but there is an easy
explanation, for, way off, fifty miles
away, at that very moment, the film-
maker, a cousin, was priming-the-pump
with questions for the first-time inter-
viewee. So be the moments of pleasure.

May 31, 2011

Neither Moth Nor Rust

On grand display at the rare book fair in Paris in 2003
eight perfectly bound copies of *Bureau de Tabac*
(Editiones Unes, 1990) in different colors, the work of second-
year (2000) students at the Ecole Estienne:

> Françoise Richard
> Anne-Laure Courtés
> Sophie Guyolot
> Emmanuelle Joseph
> Maïlys Hérubel
> Virginie Cazenove
> Emmanuelle Joseph
> Corinne Doussin

Note that there are only seven different names on the list
(Emmanuelle Joseph's appearing twice). A lapse in my note-

taking? Or was Emmanuelle a double-dipper?   I fanned the
books out so as to form a kaleidoscopic sun, like the one
Caeiro saluted each day of his life.

June 18, 2011

You Can't Write Them All, Right?

Who, finally, but Teresa Rita Lopes gets to nail it all down.
A descendant of the party in question (or is it a questionable
party?) gifts her the ms—the smoking gun—and now you
all know that my friend (more an acquaintance, really) did
have an actual life and (like us all) a living to make, and
that the poem (as indicated from the get-go) that I slipped
into the first of the only two issues of *Orpheu* that made it
into print was of his own making. Now, to cream the jest,
C's satchel turns up, with a handful of lucubrations (pristine
of publication) squirreled away against time or what you
will, by this down-on-one-knee, genuflector worshipper of
sleek motorcars furnished to the carriage trade or to others
needful of an emblem, a staff car. The Futurist takes to
business, and the shameless poet will borrow a Chevrolet.

July 31, 2011

War Games

Greater than the warrior is the historian. Hastings,
Trafalgar, Johannesburg, Sommes, Gallipoli—story
has no purchase on what happened there. If, as it is

said, the spoils may belong to the victor, but the laurel
goes elsewhere. Even the memoirist owns the burning
deck where the admiral singes to a cinder. Yet I would
think no one (especially not the English) would see
the joke in the proposal and willingly resist the urge
to prove their superior civilization by waging war.
Memories of defeat at the hands of rough Dutch
farmers fade fast; besides this time Tommie won't
have so far to go for his war games. This is no time,
no place, for a home-front game devised to let the Huns
and Brits slug it out, even up, before they make nice.

Sept. 27, 2011

Not Again (cc Heteronyms)

I'm tired of trying to be interested in the things
I'm supposed to be interested in, according to
someone else or to myself (the more frequent case)
when I think I want to be a better citizen, a more
informed being, or simply a knowing participant
in the buzz around me or, even more simply, the
gray matter in my head. *Basta. Chega.* Enough.
Three languages, it takes, if I start out by quoting
from the Italian, as Henry James did. See, I'm
showing-off again—no theatrical self-command!

Oct. 14, 2011

Don't Call

even though
you can,
courtesy of
the i-phone,
especially if
your life is
in the balance.
I say NO to
sons-of-bitches
with two cents
for a stamp or
stamped to i-pad.
Let me call you.
See if I don't.

Oct. 28, 2011

I Know Who He Is

Out of the post office he came, holding the door open for
me, and, thinking he must know me, saying hello. Thinking
I must know him, I, too, say hello, and add my thanks.
Walking around worried about myself, to see him abruptly
like that gave me heart. He looked older, heavier, but more
robust than I remembered, and just as straight. But best of all,
here he was, a survivor of cutting and stitching, a bit of proof,
walking, conducting his business with dispatch, panache.

Nov. 8, 2011

Spot of Time

A proverb—folk wisdom depreciated,
kicked to the curb by all who know—
pops up unexpectedly (if not at beck and
call), fit for duty, ready to take over my
train of thought, delivering me to my
people, to memories of conclusions—
chief means to the ends of memory—
cultivated or not. A beggar, for example,
works the metro, and before him I see my
mother, a mark for such pleading if there was
ever one, but I, her son, will not, ever, give in.

Dec. 8, 1998 / Nov. 13, 2011

122 + 96

Of course, there's nothing magical about these numbers,
standing, respectively, for the span he would have lived
so far, had he lived, and the length of time since his death.
He died in the midst of the Great War, as far away from
the trenches as Paris, in Montparnasse, fighting that held
little interest for him (if one can trust the evidence of the
documents that survive), he who was courting his own
demons. But his death (and certainly the manner of it)
shook up his friends, especially those at the end of the
Paris run, in the Rossio station, hard by the Palace Hotel,
in the Baixa. Jorge de Sena, many years later, ferreting
around in Pessoa's trunk of notes and scraps, came upon

Os Indicios de Ouro in manuscript, and was moved deeply enough to record the discovery in his diary on May 28, 1954. That is, rounding it off, nearly 58 years ago—64 after his birth day, 36 after his death.

Feb. 19, 2012

Terence, this is stupid stuff

And it is. Woe to the wag who would someday say *tanto Pessoa já enjoa.* Of course, he would not be the first one to feel that way (that was *moi*, I boast), but he was overruled (though I wasn't). Like Terence's *confrère*, I keep churning it out, always with a burden: seriousness, desperation, selflessness, irony, and (to sweeten the pot) mockery. Imperious in thought, rational as all-hell, schematic (there are always three causes, three opportunities, three roads to take) with sub-scripts and breakdown categories as needed—everything, in fact, a footnote to the grand shebang—the never reached, never named, never described, all-encompassing Notion. Still the beat goes on— all limelight with Charlot in a time-share.

Feb. 24, 2012

Many Parts

It's not so much that in a lifetime a
man plays many parts on this crust
of a stage but that he will want to play
more than one of those parts pretty
much at the same time. Masks some
call them but, in my case, they mask
nothing. If Mae teased us with "peel
me a grape," so she could eat its belly
laid bare, I say, "peel me an onion,"
and when the peeling is done, poof,
there is nothing left, nothing there, but
an essential sincerity. It's not so much
that I like it that way, but that it's so like
me: the *nada* that is nothing—the nothing
that is all the all there is. Caeiro would
have put all this better than I do, but,
foolishly, I put him down, long ago.

Mar. 1, 2012

The Lyric

The lyric outlives the heart
while the monument survives
the memory for which it stands.
No lyric will match it in its
steadfastness though memory
is the lyric's delivery system,
that fails for there are no

modest monuments, which
is why there are so many
that in the end won't help.

Mar. 1, 2012

Self-Pity

I was a figure of fun, someone to be ridiculed,
someone to be uncomfortable with, a person
without qualities that merit (surely not command)
respect, in short, a nothing that always provoked
easy laughter. Just look at that picture at Abel's
and doubt no longer that no one thought I had any-
thing to live up to. And they were right, as far as
things went, and they went nowhere that I could tell.

Mar. 3, 2012

Auspices

Would it not have surprised them,
Bernardo Soares or Vicente Guedes
(the ½ heteronym's name, if truth be
known, in a former life—no matter
what made for this change)—a surprise,
I say, to find that those depressives (no
matter how arranged, their sequence
always more or less capricious) would
serve for many as the *sortes Vergilinæ*

in the twenty-first century, the whole
shebang an observant's Sunday missal.

Mar. 13, 2012

Only This

The patient dead will not
teach patience to the living,
not having the desire or, if
truth be told, the patience.

Questions will be asked of
words written down or over-
head, but nothing will stick
to nothing, and the curious

will persist and the text will
last, elastic but unforgiving.
The lead trumps the cursive,
and that is as it should not be.

Mar. 13, 2012

King Me!

At the moment that the young Hadrian found his future in
Virgil he was so pleased that he forgot to seek out the
particulars.

The open path stretched out before him and though it would reach the British Isles, where he would plant a great wall, he hadn't a clue about the specifics, the what, who, where, when, and why.

He would know what to do and why when he came to it, a life of details modified meaningfully only by dreams.

Long story short, he came to fancy himself a God-maker, and put his shoulder to the wheel to make it happen.

But herein he failed, the forces of history being what they are, and, of course, through no fault of his own he failed.

The moral: a capacious vision is never enough ipso facto to make a go of it.

Mar. 13, 2012

There?

Birds in Lisbon?
There were birds?
Where were those
birds? Oh, yes,
now I remember.
There was one,
but alas it was
no ibis.

Mar. 14, 2012

Two for the Books

1. Too good to be true?
Not at all. Italians still
shop at the *tabacchi* for
pens, bus tickets, stamps,
for cigarettes and other
smokes when they fear
they are running out.
Once, in Paris (so goes
the story) a young student
locked in on a word so very
like his own name in the title
of a poem versified from a
language he did not yet know.
The rest? The rest is history.
2. *Cruz na porta da tabacaria!*
(Grant me this rhetorical flourish,
for no longer will a family nail a
cross to a door to signal a death.)
No matter. Gone now is the teller
of the vagarious story, a man of
words who (for ever and a day)
espoused a language, married a
country, and became a poet.

Apr. 19, 2012

Tomorrow 2

Always one more day
(except for the last one
when tomorrow is no
longer the new today).

Apr. 20, 2012

Same Difference; or Everyone's Call

Whitman hears *death* in the sound
the sea makes and finds it *delicious*.
Nevermore is the sound Poe coaxes
from a raven and cannot get enough
of it. In the buzz of bees Burt extracts
an admonition: *work while you can*.

Apr. 25, 2012

Wednesday

Never checked this out, but obviously, this
is not the first time my birthday falls on a
Wednesday. Still I think it all too appropriate
for I am Wednesday's child—full of care and
woe—the one faced with nothing but defeat,
calamity, loss. The feather falls, he said, and
hope evaporates. All this occurs posthumously,
in memoriam, a case of self-absorbed complaint

that turns to noise that turns away its audience.
Here we go again... *Hieronymo's mad againe.*

June 13, 2012

Wisdom is Woe

Success perverts,
so does failure.

Aug. 31, 2012

Daddy Long-legs

thinks not of a long run,
building and rebuilding
as necessary, time and
again in the course of the
untimed day. It knows
when to abandon, starting
up elsewhere after a careless
swipe brings all to disaster
to the canvas as it stands.

Sept. 2, 2012

Lesson Learned

Scene in an old movie, either before or after 1935:
a hunched-over patron (old before his time) drinks
and sketches away at the bar. We don't know what
he is sketching until in a flash of self-knowledge and
despair he crumples up his sketch and throws it away.
Somebody (maybe the bartender, no, another patron)
picks it up, and the crumpled sketch shows forth, in a
rough but perfect oval, the line drawing of a headshot.
Long story short, the sketcher is discovered, hired by
a manufacturer, and becomes an unlikely success when
his throw-away woman becomes the oval-bar face of
the firm's oval-bar soap. Moral: throw nothing away,
but if you do, cast it before someone with wherewithal.

Sept. 10, 2012

Regression Analysis

I remember explaining in a letter to someone
or other that when I was despondent and could
write nothing else, I wrote in "my book." It was
as if I were in an obscure place in a dark dream
facing a black forest of thick trees and all that
I could do was fall into that forest and chop away
at a tree I could not measure or even see clearly.
Each time it was a different tree though many
of them were similar enough to the next one that
even though I saw the similarity right off the bat
I could not turn away. Now all those recorded

attempts at getting down those thoughts are
treated like ingots of gold and lined up, ordered,
arranged and rearranged, annotated and put forth
into a world that will not or cannot discriminate.
Out of my pain I did not make poetry. That's hard
for the believers to believe, but of course it's true.

Sept. 11, 2012

For the Love of Mike

The plan came to me when I
should have been sleeping was
to start out my day by writing
something about Pessoa's *O
Banqueiro Anarquista.* But I
was sidetracked, for I turned
first to the obituary page in the
New York *Times* and found
that Mike was gone. Then and
there my original plan was
scuttled, and I turned to think-
ing about Mike, someone who
had wanted nothing more than
his human rating to be taken
as a public intellectual. Of
salience in this regard is the
Times detail that a biographer
of "fruity lefties" (his words,
not mine) had bombarded
the *Times* with letters that

had gone unpublished. Piles
of them that Mike himself
named "Wreszin Discards."
Now that's a thought, a
compendium of letters once
deemed unfit to print.

Sept. 16, 2012 / Apr. 8, 2016

Repurposed

I've been repurposed so often that
I've very nearly lost my posthumous
way. Or is it merely that the wayward
possibilities of using a man's words
when he couldn't make up his mind
as to what he intended by them opens
the door to exploitation? After all is
said and done, my case may just be
that of a grouse, like Thomas Stearns
Eliot, who dumped his bitching on
Ezra, that egregious redhead, and
voilá, from shards, *The Waste Land.*

Sept. 22, 2012

Keepers of Sheep

In the only conversation we ever had
he told me that he was the caretaker of

the farm down the road and that the farm
had just recently stocked up on sheep,
which added to his overall caretaking duties
in that they now included caring for them
but that he wouldn't be caring for sheep
much longer because his boss had hired a
shepherd from Lisbon, who should be
arriving any day now. I think Rossio, Black
Horse Square, Caeiro, but I don't push it.

Sept. 22, 2012

Guest List

You can't get started any too soon, I say, even if your next
birthday is not the 125th, which mine is. In fact, I already feel
rushed. I must get started on the invitations list since getting it
right will certainly take more than one stab at it. So here goes.
First of all, Adolfo Casais Monteiro, whose nosiness helped me
launch that whopper about the near-big-bang birth of the
heteronyms, João Gaspar Simões, whose plodding, earnest
careerism celebrated me early, promoted me late, to the end,
not José Régio (well-meaning, but a pain) or Miguel Torga
(despite his having lamented me at my death by closing his
office and strolling about in nearby woods), Carlos Queiros,
who treated me like family and piped praise over the radio
when I died, Luís de Montalvor, who built his own career by
publishing my books, not Ronald de Carvalho, who pretty
much forgot me when he returned to Brazil and who couldn't
care much about my posthumous reputation, Antonio Ferro,
who for personal and political reasons kept up his friendship to

the end, Almada Negreiros, who always up-staged me (and himself), Côrtes-Rodrigues, whose true sentiments lay with the folk, Pierre Hourcade, the first to translate my poems into French, Ilda Stichini, whose 1930s act included a declamation of *O menino da sua mãe*, which should have given me a greater boost at the time than it did, Elizabeth Bishop, who scotched her classmate Mary McCarthy's malicious plan to promote Willemsen's attack on Edwin Honig, Jorge de Sena, who inadvertently identified himself as my "accountant" by putting everything he ever wrote about me into two volumes with the all-too-appropriate title of *Fernando Pessoa & Cª Heterónima*, Eduardo Lourenço, who ventured to publish his wealth of scholarly thought without footnotes, Octavio Paz, who struck the bell for me, loud and clear, with a single essay, Jonathan Griffin, Armand Guibert, Edwin Honig, Peter Rickard, Zenith, and Quintanilha—let these few represent all the earnest translators of the work, José Augusto Seabra, who despite his servility to Parisian semiotics managed to say some interesting things about some poems, Jerónimo Pizarro, who combines a prophet's zeal with elbow grease, Maria Aliete Galhoz, who sniffed out the rubai poems after Alexandrino Severino tracked one down in a journal, Martins Garcia, who got a doctorate out of Northrup Frye and me, Teresa Rita Lopes, who saw the surviving papers early and was keen enough to copy many of them, Teresa Sobral Cunha, who kept on despite being mercilessly plagiarized as well as frozen out by Assírio & Alvim, José Blanco, perhaps the most disinterested dedicated scholar of them all, Jacinto do Prado Coelho, whose idea was that I personally had my cake and ate it heteronymically, that lesser Monteiro, who keeps putting English words in my mouth, H. D. Jennings, who after his retirement learned the language so that he could read and write about me in South

Africa, Robert Brechon, who frenchified my *oeuvre* as befits
the Pléiade writer that I am, Angel Crespo, who should have
worn gloves when touching the cenotaph, the touch was that
hot, Luciana and Cleonice, *grande dames*, one of whom
confesses to all that she's in love with Álvaro, and the other
who knew that there was always more than enough F. P. to
satisfy the demand, Onésimo, who smoked out the strategy of
mythos, Maria Irene Ramalho, who took note of Portugal's
westward look on Europe's map and wrote a book, Susan
Brown, whose knowledge was passed on to Harold Bloom,
who swallowed it whole but misattributed it to Maria Irene,
Arnaldo, who shut down *Persona* way too soon. Must not
forget Ofélia, steadfast, true, silent to the core. Well, best to
stop there, at least for the nonce, and let all others with a
legitimate claim sit at the children's table, where they will sit
with Santa Rita Pintor, Mike (my British half-brother) and Sá
Carneiro. For many others important to me on a daily basis—
Abel or the *galegos* (and their caged crows), who ran a bar tab
for me and several others—sorry, there's no more room at the
inn. That's enough for today—stop, before I go English, that is
to say, ironic.

Sept. 22, 2012

MacGuffins

When Elizabeth threw in her lot with by-chance
friends in Brazil, she could hardly have thought
that she was not replicating, in any sense, the life
of Ricardo Reis. Of course, she didn't know the
language but her some-French would certainly

be of help. When Ricardo (and not even his
fellow heteronyms had the impertinence to call
him that) shook off Lisbon, he left no forwarding
address, no longer wishing, apparently, to keep
up appearances with his Luso acquaintances.
Even his illusionary progenitor lost track of him,
something that happened as soon as the ship sailed
away, out of sight from the Lisbon *cais*. Did
he step ashore in Rio or somewhere north of
the then capital of the Ilha de Vera Cruz (as
the country was once called, or did Santos serve
as the port of entry for this saturnine poet—never
to leave Brazil until Saramago brought him back
to Lisbon as a way to settle long-standing accounts
of some mysterious sort or other? Of Elizabeth's
life in Brazil we know everything (or nearly every-
thing), of Ricardo Reis's we know not a thing.
General João Figueiredo, after 6 years as Brazil's
President, advised his countrymen to grant him
his one wish: "Just forget me." Heartsick advice,
beside the point. Forgotten? Not on your life.

Sept. 24, 2012

I, Too, Have Lived

I, too, have lived among the dead,
not merely the dead who have left us
their books, their music, their art, or
the defunct members of our families
or that coterie of friends (unnamed

here but so fulsomely lamented by
Álvaro). Rather those many others,
the unknown dead that Whitman
addressed (with shameless self-love),
the yet-unborn readers who could
look for him under their boot soles.
If my soul mate too soon became
but a vivid *memento mori*, immortal
to me till my own end (and beyond,
if my ephebes count at all), what
could I say about the early and even
greater loss to me of my Master?
Quoth the Lisbon bookman, *não, não
temos, mas já tivemos nesta casa.*

Sept. 26, 2012

Same Old

It's just the old habit, this sitting down to write
without a single thought to begin with. Still, it's
a living even though the newspapers pay little
(when they pay) and journals and periodicals (at
least the kind in which I collaborate) nothing at all.
And in the latter case publication in an inaugural
issue turns out in most cases not to be even a pitiable
investment since they so often shoot their load right
then and there with that debut—then, poof, they are
heard from no more. (Check the facsimile series
for their modest resurrection these so many decades
later.) Why this oh so late lament when all that was

so lost is now so, prodigally, found? Isn't this bill
of ancient dolor, like so much that I write, merely
a result of habit, one that may or may not result in
um bom resultado or any *resultado* at all?

Sept. 27, 2012

Counting the Candles

Literary folk and other folks interested in literature
(for profit or gain or selfish pleasure, no matter) will
know this: O'Neill and T. S. Eliot (and I) were born
in 1888, respectively, in New York, St. Louis, and
Lisboa. Surely there were other scribbling worthies
who first saw the light of day that year, but these
are the three that come to mind at this moment.
The first one became a great dramatist, the second
an earnest dramatist, and the third one convinced him-
self that everything was drama, including his silence.
All three are claimed for Modernism by those who
decide such matters, a rubric which they would or
would not have agreed with if the term meant being
up-to-date in New York or Lisboa or Kansas City.
Three winners of the Nobel Prize for Literature—
oops, not Pessoa (though any one of my big three
merited it). No big whoops, though, for, as the poet
so famously said, *Well, we have come this far.*

Sept. 27, 2012

200

Still Life

To write the poem of the moment in
which nothing happens, I could not
do. Caeiro could, and so he did it.

Sept. 28, 2012

Don't be Interested or Curious

How is that one can spend a
lifetime worrying about final
things without ever knowing
their number, and to do so while
all the while trying to avoid
splitting infinitives or ending
sentences with prepositions?
There's hardly time left to worry
over the distinct possibility that
when NASA cranks its vehicle
to the top of that mountain on
Mars the vehicle will just topple
down into a crevasse and not have
sense enough to cry out for help.
Or, another question, shouldn't we
worry some about what will come
of that baby—Elizabeth Polizzi's—
you know—Jersey's Snooki?

Sept. 29, 2012

Closing

So Cavalcanti of Brazil has discovered, on
the analogy (presumably) of Hadrian and his
Antinous, that I had a lover in my room the
night I rounded the bend in the road. Ofélia,
he says, spent the night at my side. News to
me. Had he suggested Campos, I'd have said
maybe, as a way to call attention to my work.
Sad, though, if truth be known, he wasn't there
either, though he would have been of greater
use than Ofélia—to talk to the doctor, my cousin,
who scootched away right after I expired, or to
the good nurses, who, of course, had better things
to do than stand around contemplating the dead.
No, they left me by myself, and since I had
known that my stay in hospital would be short,
I had come there with little or no preparation. As
it happened, my rather surprising death provided
all the drama I deserved, though in the scheme
of things it was hardly a blip in the quotidian
life of the denizens working the French hospital.
Had I known my disappearance was imminent,
however, I'd have foreseen the poetic nicety
of a death—mine— taking place, not there, but
in the English hospital conveniently placed just
that long stone's throw away from my room
off the stairwell in my sister's house.

Sept. 30, 2012

Unfolding in Particulars

Ripeness is all—cribbed by the mariner;
but nowhere do I ever mention Melville (at
least I don't think so). The so-called 1920s
"discovery" of his writing never reached me
in Lisbon, even though the news of it blew
the doors off the salons of the better literary
circles of London, and I *was* a reader of the
Times, the *Athenaeum*, and maybe one other
journal. But what does Melville mean to say
by this? Is he being positive? negative?
Ripeness is the acme, the fulfillment, some-
thing to strive for? Or is the end pint, since,
as we know, ripeness (in fruit, e. g.) brushes
through the moment of its (the fruit's) fall
from the tree or bush into a consummation
of decay? Tell it, tell it, I say, to a last leaf.

Oct. 2, 2012

Agua no bico?

Yes, guilty as charged,
but I never carried water
for anyone, not if I could
help it. Fate saved me
from the librarian's job
up the coast, way up in
Cascais. I think they
were the first to question

my English competence
(though I'm not sure
about that, since only
behind your back do
people say such things).
Of course, it is much
easier to denigrate my
English poems than
to have written them.
But, of course, I tell
this to the marines.

Oct. 3, 2012

Sá-Carneiro, for Starters

With a little help from his friends
Ted Hughes translated him, and
Ted's friends (well, one of them)
told me that young Ted and his
wife (when the four were neighbors)
actually may have "begun to trans-
late Pessoa." But there's no evidence
to indicate that they actually did so.
Pity. More the merrier, I always
say. But *minha patria é a língua
portuguesa*, Bernardo Soares used
to say. People always take that as
evidence that I am very loyal to
Portugal, which is to conflate
messengers. My utterance would

have stopped with the word *lingua*,
meaning that it was my tongue
(a metonym? a synecdoche?) that
was, strictly speaking, my native
land. Right there was confusion.
For though I had two languages
at the ready, I made do, as most
will do, with one tongue. That's
where I lived, on and off my *língua*,
herding words against the jihads.
As for Sá-Carneiro's poems, I had
them for years, intending (always)
to gather them in a collective book,
but arrangements for publication
always fell through, and, some say
before my time, that I failed, too.
The irony, to put it bluntly, is that
some think that my disappearance
in 1935 enabled Sá-Carneiro to
debut triumphantly. Well, maybe
so. After all, Sena said that it was
Mário's early death which made it
possible for me to be the poet I
became. Perhaps, but I hate to
think so. And having said that,
I appeal to the existence of my
coterie of up-standing, stand-
alone, talky 'nyms. By the way,
will somebody bother to check
out the context in which I spoke
(some say misspoke)—unwisely,

perhaps—I put that shibboleth
out there for grabs, an agenda?

Oct. 5, 2012

Sometimes

Sometimes I think that the obituary
page in the New York *Times* is pre-
pared just for me. Occasionally, I
feel (slightly) embarrassed by what
others may call my *schadenfreude*.
But the page means a lot of things to
me, including proving out a timeline.
Strange, though, I never check the
weather, nowhere. The channel that
deals exclusively with weather is just
a T.V. place I sometimes stumble into
but can't wait to get away from. No
doubt about it. History beats Guess.

Oct. 9, 2012

Trinity

You and everybody else know who these women
are. The one who was murdered and later exhumed
and morbidly crowned, the religious who loved too
well and was jilted by the French officer lover, and
the queen whose lie to her husband was backed up

by divine interference. Is there further proof (beyond
the fact that women get short shrift in my work) that
I was a misogynist? Any more so than Campos, who
dallied about with Daisy, or Ricardo Reis, who had no
greater use for the women he addressed in his poems,
those whose portion of reality lies in the mention of
their names in a line of verse or two?. How cheeky
of that garlanded novelist to give that affected dandy
with his attitude and degree a hotel maid for a lover!

Oct. 10, 2012

Math

That was my game, the division of cells
in two, over and again. Every thought
parsed into parts, and those parts parsed
again. Any wonder that with so much
division in the offing that I, too, would
divide into selves. Too bad my every
self didn't divide itself as well so that
we could let go, glyphs in the clouds.

Oct. 12, 2012

Tarzan

Tarzan made the scene one hundred years ago.
Edgar Rice Burroughs never set foot in Africa.
With the exception of a couple of months or so

at the University of Lisbon, the whole of FP's
formal education took place in Africa. He wrote
a lot, as did Burroughs, but he never wrote about
Africa, though sleuths—well, one of them—has
tracked the traces of light he recalled in the *Ode
Marítima* as blinking off Lisbon quays to faint
memories of slivers and fragments of minerals
showing forth from wharf planks in Durban.
Odd what a boy takes in but loses to memory
that the poet in him brings forth when needed.
Ah, had the *mapa cor-de-rosa* scheme worked
out for the Lusos, Tarzan's dad would not have
been Lord Greystoke but some Lisbon bloke
who'd never back down in a bully face off;
and (you bet) the futurist ultimatum would've
stung attentive ears (as, of course, it did not).

Oct. 12, 2012

Nothing to Add

Of course there's nothing to add,
nothing to add since there was
nothing of substance there to begin
with, as if I cared anyway. Writing
was a way of being in the world, of
the world, a way to call attention to
myself in cafes and offices, without
having people bother me, feeling
that naturally I must attend to them.
But I saved every scrap, every scratch-

pad note, every word written hurriedly
on the back of an old invoice or spare
letterhead. It didn't much matter
since it was just my way of seeming
to be productive. But I bit the apple
and began to publish screeds and
polemical pieces. And pretty soon
I couldn't stop, as I dug into the
saved papers to see what I could
salvage, rewrite, and send off so
that I could see my name in print.
This was a case, now that I think
about it, of Pessoa being Pessoa,
of Pessoa trying to be a person.
Well, that's the way I look at it.
Sometimes

Oct. 15, 2012

Not Possibly

On the date of his birth (set down by his whacky
deliverer long after the already retroactive fact),
a professor offers his cautiously couched opinion
that Campos is "possibly the greatest poet who
never lived." Never lived? Take your cue from
the poet who 150 years ago rhetorically asked a
then-somebody if her verse did "breathe," knowing
the truth. Her word, her bond, asked for no surety.

Oct. 15, 2012

Everyman

Every man his own poet, a
shibboleth promoted by the
Sage of Concord, is rivaled
only by the Sage's own call
for poetry resulting from a
meter-making argument.
Yet while he was never guilty
of criticizing a single poem
by any *everyman* at all, he
rather routinely violated his
catchy precept. Without ever
attending to the poetry made
by *everyman*, he fell under
the spell of boxing his verse
out in quatrains—unlike the
elitist that is Pessoa, lining
up names to stock the coterie
of poets licensed to ring damn
near all possible changes. It's
a fact that no poem by *every-
man* made it into *Parnassus*.
You could look it up. So I
repeat myself? *e dai*?

Oct. 17, 2012

Correspondence

His business letters, full of details of negotiations, display-
his aptitude for the basics of arithmetic. His courtship letters
are those of a rather silly old *melado*. His breakup letters
are forceful, canny, full of misdirection, and amusing in
a gallows-humor sort of way (but of course they are written
by Campos, the sidekick, who at the drop of a hat took on
whatever dirty work Fernando was faced with). His public
letters to newspapers and journals often exuded superiority
or supercilious courtesy. When he wrote to the boys at
presença, knowing who buttered his bread, he played nice.
Encouraged by questions from Casais Monteiro, he mainly
told biographical stretchers. He got away scot free in letters
back to Durban school officials, in which he portrayed him-
self as a concerned psychiatrist just trying to do his job.
Make no mistake. In his letters he was no Eça, no Garrett
or Herzog, or even Abigail Van Buren. Not his cup of tea.

Oct. 21, 2012

No Boat

That's how Marianne's friend,
Margaret, was listed in the

Marblehead Yacht Club registry
of members. One sailing craft

not to worry about in case of
weather, one person not expected

at lectures on the particular joys
of boats and other small craft.

No sailing merrily downstream for
the likes of Margaret or Marianne.

No boat for Pessoa either, and he
probably didn't know how to drive

and certainly had no car, yet the poet
in him did fancy the car metaphor.

In a drive to Sintra, in the curve in
the road, he saw life and death, the

unfolding unknown and the known,
wedded and knotted from the get-go.

Oct. 23, 2012

I Say

Maybe it's because Lélia face-booked a photo
of herself standing next to the familiar figure
before *A Brasileira*, maybe it's because Lélia
hails from the isle of Santa Catarina, and may-
be it has nothing to do with these, but, I say,
it's time to elevate this statue in the sacred via
of the Chiado to the heights enjoyed by Saint
James holding forth in his Catedral de Santiago
de Compostela. If this be seen as an egregious

act of poaching among the flora in the forests
of hagiography, well, let us get on with it.

Oct. 27, 2012

The Back Story

I knew, as a friend, I had to help him,
though we never ran into one another,
never met at the Martinho da Arcada
to dine, to raise a glass to one another's
health and two or three more to our
memories and missing friends, to
reminisce about those months in our
callow youth (as least I was callow)
when we planned and put out *Orpheu*,
and as the Director of S.N.I. I knew
how to do it. Just the ticket was the
new Antero de Quental poetry prize,
I told him—in a letter, of course, that
I gently advised him to destroy.
And he must have done so, for you
won't find that letter or any others
relating to the caper among his papers
at the Library. Naturally, I destroyed
his side of the correspondence as well.
Anything that smacked of a handout
was out of the question. He wouldn't
have tolerated that from me (or anyone
else, for that matter), but a prize that
one might win, fair and square, that

was a horse of a different color. So
So I coached him. The prize would
go to a single poem, running to at
least one hundred pages and broadly
patriotic in character. Couldn't he
build such a poem around the cluster
of poems historical in bent like the
ones that I had read in a journal some
years back? That was my suggestion
and he ran with it. I sent him some
money (of my own) to pay the printer
that I had brought in to help play out
the scheme. I helped the poet deploy
his poems generously so as to make
up a book of one hundred pages if
you counted the pages in the way I
instructed the printer to print them.
So far so good—a bit shaky this way
of counting, yet I'd make it work if
it came down to it. But it all very
nearly came a-cropper, when, to my
great surprise the judges awarded the
prize elsewhere. I couldn't override
their decision, of course, but I could
take the chance of declaring that there
would be two first prizes, and did so.
I also scraped up money enough to
cover the two awards equally. There
was no criticism of this in the papers,
not because it was not widely noticed
that I had had some hand in the game
but because S.N.I. was very effective

in slicing, dicing the newspapers until
any whiff of such tricks was made to
go away. But that's not to say that I
got off scot-free, which I did not. I
was called on the carpet, and came this
close to losing my job. But I didn't.
Want to know more? Talk to Blanco.
By the way, have you seen my copy of
Mensagem, so graciously inscribed?

Oct. 27, 2012

Obits

It is not that one needs to be called
to thoughts of his mortality but first
thing I check each and every morning,
sometimes even before showering, are
the obituaries in the New York *Times*.
I'm no fanatic in the contemplation
of the evidences of what used to be
called the common doom, but I will
not forgo this quotidian reality check.
How I envied the sloe-eyed vacationer
at the Algarve beach, for example,
who, dripping wet, as he climbed the
stairs, was greeted by a someone or
other rushing up to him and gushing
out excitedly, "he died, he's dead."

No comforting words, no name blurted,
only the last news of one more down.

Nov. 1, 2012

No Way

Well if he wasn't Italian and he wasn't born
on the Portuguese mainland, what was he?
I need to know. Of course, in my time there
was not yet this pile of scared-up evidence
to indicate that Columbus belonged to our
history, to our mythology. Why, though, I ask,
would we want primacy in the discovery of the
Americas? The Corte-Reais, after all, followed
on the heels of the Vikings—well no, they didn't.
The Vikes were there, walking around, centuries
before. And, of course, Columbus didn't know
where he came ashore, calling those islands in
the Caribbean, the Indies. Now, Vasco da Gama
(and others) did sail to India (a little later than
the others, but close enough) and that other dude,
sailing for Spain (you know the one, who got
himself killed off on the way), did start out as
the commander of ships that (in a coinage that
stuck) "circumnavigated the globe" Well Colon
didn't get into *Mensagem*. And in my book he
didn't belong, not even via a dismissive note.

Nov. 8, 2012

Neither Chick Nor Child

I read in the *Times* the obituary for
William Faulkner's biographer, a
someone the founding-father of county
Yoknapatawpha called his "spiritual
Son"; and it gets me thinking. Was it
just that Pessoa did not live long enough
to have a spiritual son or two that he did
not have a spiritual son or two? Not so
much, I think. For that matter, neither
did his heteronyms. Like him, they never
married. And if Ricardo Reis did knock-
up that hotel maid in Lisbon, the dirty
deed took place in somebody else's pipe-
dream. No, in Pessoa's imagined sphere
there was no room for progeny of any
sort, spiritual or genetic, or wives either.
These boys were loners, sometimes
going their merry way, sometimes not,
but ever solitary, always *isolato* losers.

Nov. 24, 2012

Century and a Quarter

2013 marks the next major
anniversary, and who knows
what flurry will come about:
all those many one-or-two-
step-up platforms holding up

long tables fronted stem to stern
by a sentinel row of potted plants
or buckets of cut flowers and man-
ned by a mini-bevy of experts or
noted appreciators, each one alert
to tell all, by turn, what the poet
means to us, has meant to others,
and how, in his time, he was ignored,
etc., etc., and so forth. Its truth lies
in its reenactment of what was once
a first enactment, the single virtue
of which resided in its being useful
in itself, not by its being any sort of
bridge to somewhere else, a step
forward to god-knows-where, but
a step forward, to be sure.

Nov. 24, 2012

Chega? No, Not Yet

"Too much has been written,"
you will say, "and even more
has been said, over and over."
But I plead the case, "has the
right thing been said, at the
right time, so as to please me?"
No, thank the gods, for at such
a moment, there would be first

a pause, billowing into silence,
and then a slow turning away.

Nov. 25, 2012

At Long Last

Victor Mendes has colorized
him! Like a still from an old
movie, fit for reviewing by all,
including those fastened to the
grainy blacks and grays of yester-
year. Look, though, no color can
take away the sure gait or stride
of the man of counterfeit affairs
on his way to or from his day.

Nov. 28, 2012

Ekphrasis

The infamous photo snapped at Abel's,
a copy of which he inscribed to Ofélia
in compliance with a request—*Fernando
Pessoa in flagrante delitro*—is both
candid and staged. In it, a poseur has
pushed back his hat, unbuttoned his coat,
and buried his left hand in his pants pocket
(fingering his money to see if he has the
coin enough to cover another go). Funny,

though, he also runs a tab at Abel's. In short,
he would have others see him as just one of
the boys, nipping away on company time.

Dec. 3, 2012

The Critic

he who, it seems, must be quoted all the time
in certain places,
he who swallowed whole the poet's *blague*
detailing the birth of the heteronyms,
he who translated directly from the Russian
words by Dostoyevsky without knowing Russian
and then acknowledging that the notebooks (his
source) had never been available for perusal,
he who threw a hissy fit when he felt neglected
at Coimbra,
he who was shorter (even in intellect) than anyone
imagined,
he who took shamelessly from others but was disdainful of the
quotation mark (chapter and verse available on request),
he who, self-satisfied, sat in judgment but brooked
no criticism of himself,
he who is the shameless one who need not be named evermore

Dec. 4, 2012

Ockham

It's simpler to kick the can down the road
than it is to dispose of a razor.

Dec. 6, 2012.

Milestones, Not Millstones

At five score and four he soldiers
on, dieting on green bananas.

Dec. 11, 2012

Le plus change

As guys get older and things around them change,
they lament the loss of better times, better friends,
better toys. However, it is only because they have
not yet discovered (but may never discover) the
poet who will or has already incorporated those
changes in poetry. It has ever been so, and it is so
still again, whether the old guy catches on or not.

Dec. 22, 2012

Admissible

What I hoped for was reasonable, honest
appraisal, but boundless praise is better.

Dec. 25, 2012

The Question

Were these lives worth living?
Don't ask. Better not. You'll
pay in regrets if you do. Let
me explain, if I may. Well…
oh, forget it. It's not worth
thinking about. Shush…
forget it… mum's the word.

Dec. 30, 2012

Casa

It's a meritocracy, this thing of each *fado* singer of any worth
      having a "house."
I suppose it's tantamount to a poet's domination in some café
      or other.
The singer and poet share this having a stage and, if they are
      lucky, attention and silence.
I always had competitors, though, and thus was almost never
      the single focus of a table-centered café.

Well, it didn't matter; after all, the single solitary reaper sang
       alone, sang to herself, and didn't care when no one
       heard her.
At least I, who never thought to frame the question, can only
       think it was ever so.

Jan. 2, 2013

Now, At Long Last

—something I thought I would
never see—a New York *Times*
notice of a new Saramago novel
in which the reviewer does not
show off by referring to Pessoa.

Jan. 6, 2013

Attention Will be Paid

Some day they will gauge my meaning and competence
by determining at just what time by my personal clock I
scrawled away on each scrap of paper I left behind. Some
of them will be pretty accurate, traced minutely through a
minute examination of my script, just when and how brandy
in my blood drove the cursive shapes from my hand.

Jan. 9, 2013

Apocrypha

Can you ever
make up for the
past? Anyone?
Ever? Try it.
Try again.

Jan. 11, 2013

Obras

They say that the *obras de Mafra*
are done but I think they've just been
scaled back. My *obras*? No scaling
back. They are still in the making.
There is something thunderous and
ponderous, visionary, hopeful, and
tragic at one and the same moment,
about the unfinished masterwork—
the symphony, the epic, the cathedral,
the palace—that enthralls more purely
than any work finished to the nines.

Jan. 24, 2013

Exceptionalism

Only the Lusos would come up with this one.
The national trait nonpareil is *saudade*, a term

and a notion with no precise equivalent in any
of the known languages, past or present or (to
jack it up) future—*saudade,* the word for things
missing, lost or—the kicker—never experienced
at all. Ah Sebastião, the missing non-*retornad*o,
incapable of future failure, never to be put
to the test, the beau ideal of *saudosismo.*

Jan. 25, 2013

Better Believe It

More people interpret his *Mensagem* than
have actually read it. He wrote the poem
but never had the temerity to even hint at
what it means. But I suspect this is true
when it comes to all writers of books with
healthy shelf-lives, like *The Odyssey, The
Divine Comedy, Faust, Hamlet, The Waste
Land.* Good company, no? The good
maker always counts on the shibboleth
that what the maker builds cannot but be
better than the maker will ever know. Of
course this is only his attempt at bluster,
a façade thrown up against the truth of
reality when it chooses to rear its head.

Jan. 26, 2013

D. M.-F.

He knew no Saul he need placate.
He was a ladies-man, always on
the lookout. Even without a single
peek at Ofélia's letters, he took her
side. I'm guessing now, but I'll bet
he couldn't abide the first Ophelia's
egregious *mauviette* of a boyfriend.

Mar. 1, 2013

That Poor Little Rich Man

Only when I learned that Nietzsche,
even while writing about the good
and virtuous lust for power and the
superlative acts native to the *uber-*
mensch was a sniveling, diseased
wreck wrapped in a threadbare robe,
unable to find heat enough to warm
him up him was I able to see in me
the potential to be a man of strength
and overwhelming power. *O mal de*
muitos, I always say, and have come
to embrace it, count on its blessings.

Mar. 5, 2013

Regrets

They've looked in vain. There is no diary.
Well, nothing beyond those lists of early
reading, which don't count. I never thought
of doing even a fake one, that could have
been attributed to *ele-mesmo* or one of the
of heteronyms. *Livro do Desassossego*? No,
that was something else, and of course I wasn't
able, finally, to give it its proper shape, or even
to finish writing it (if I could ever have been
free of it, that is). My, my, there were scraps of
writing that I couldn't decide whether to assign
to him or attribute elsewhere. You can imagine
the headache of trying to keep the whole enter-
prise straight in my head, let alone cobbling
the whole shebang together. Now, I'm talking
about the whole works, the *opera* (including
the dozens upon dozens of heteronyms I gave
names to and set aside until I could pay them
the attention due them as poets and thinkers).

Mar. 9, 2013

Love and Death

A puppet show—that's
it, two puppets and one
adept at pulling strings.
The show worked until a
string broke and right off

the performance was out
of kilter, unraveling until
it shut down. Punch and
Judy, buffetings and mean
words, harshness swathed
in sentiments *melados*, silly
maneuverings, all evasive.
A puppet must not drink,
not socially, never solo.
Annoying, isn't it, how I
keep coming back to this,
like a dog to its… *Basta*.

Mar. 9, 2013

Spinning Wheels

Frost defined literature, simply,
as "words that have become

deeds." *Simply* is my word,
not his. He would never take

a transcendental leap to "words
are deeds." There's the problem

of "metaphor," where knowledge
and art and something else meet

(that "something else" beyond
even the God particle, a true

sine qua non in these cases, to fill
out the odd-man-out trio). Would

he (now I'm talking about Pessoa),
had he the quiet time to do so

(he was wont to say), would he,
without his customary timidity,

have taken on the question, again
risking a failure of confidence?

Mar. 10, 2013

No Northern Lights

I would dare you (scholars included) to
find the word *igloo* anywhere in my

published work or, for that matter, in my
papers bunched in the trunk. After all,

for most of my life I lived in temperate
zones, and even though the hot sands

where the mother's little soldier dies and
rots show up in the poetry, there is no

frozen north, never. Indeed, even though
I saw Caeiro as a shepherd of the Walter

Mitty sort, I did not much fancy the stars
under which, as a contemplative man, he

must have pondered. No, nothing north
of mid-Germany for me, and even then

the land of Goethe was useful mainly to my
wish to beat up on the Allies. After all,

even Faust's poet took his desires to Italy,
the land of Europe's spiritual promiscuity.

Mar. 11, 2013

Arquipélago? nem de visita.

As for living there, forget it.
But had I lived there, I'd have
sat on a single island, like
Robinson Crusoe, and tended
to my knitting or, as Candide
has it, to my very own garden.
After all, if you've seen one
island, as they say, you have
seen them all. Oh, how I
sweated that time when I
labored up the coastal route
to Cascais. More evidence?
Check out Álvaro de Campos
trying to motor the way to Sintra.

You say my maternal ancestry
links us to Terceira? Forget it.

Mar. 29, 2013

Not in Defiance

Irony, perhaps, is the supreme human invention,
though it's likely that other animals sense it, too.
The galaxy, the universe (which is the larger, I
don't care) does well, very well, without it. I,
of course, prefer not to, to quote the Scrivener.

Apr. 20, 2013

Desassossego in Another Country

> *Levamos ao conhecimento*
> *de nossos amigos e freguezes*
> *que, desde o dia 17 do corrente,*
> *deixou de ser nosso viajante o*
> *sr. Bernardo Soares.*
> > *O Estado de S. Paulo*
> > 9/26/1914-9/27/1914

When he moved to his next country, that
is, Portugal, he adopted the name *Vicente
Guedes*. But that didn't last and he soon
went back to his real name, sure that the
notoriety resulting from the circumstances

surrounding the loss of his travelling sales-
men's job in Brazil wasn't worth the sham.
No more being on the road for him. A
quiet job as an assistant bookkeeper in the
Lisbon *Baixa* would suit him fine, to a T.
How comforting, too, to take lunch and
dinner at the same familiar restaurant and
not depend on catch-as-catch-can fare.

Apr. 22, 2013

Carlos Queiros

The *portador* of the infamous photo of a portly poet
drinking his cognac at Abel's to the relative who had
enjoyed her bitter-sweet moment as a poet's *namorada*
and the *porta-voz* on the radio memorializing his just
defunct poetic better is sputteringly remembered today
for a few honest poems, though the collective volumes
issued by the Montalvor-fathered Ática years ago did
little to recoup for this man, gone at forty-two, that
blush of fame that flashed-out with his own demise.

May 9, 2013

On the Vine

It's not that he put the idea into my head,
for I'd thought about it for some time; yet
he expressed it early, in a letter meant to

be encouraging in a cajoling way (cheekily
put to an older man he pretended to call
the Master), for I was (I thought) still in
mid-career with much work still to do,
poems to write, books to organize. Of
course, it was the honor (and recognition)
that came with the prize, but I thought a lot,
too, of the money—and the trip to meet the
committee and be garlanded by the King of
Sweden. But they don't honor the dead and
by the time I'd have qualified for consideration
(by my lights, of course) I'd have long since
disappeared. Casais Monteiro, canny guy that
he was, smoked me out on that occasion, but
not only then, if the truth be known. *Drill a
man, fill him with gunpowder, and let him
explode at his leisure.* So said the American
Melville. But, for me? I had run out of time.

May 14, 2013

The F♪s, etc.

I was shooting for seventy, a long-enough run
that was not out of the question. Moderately
good health tempered by a taste for red wine
and inexpensive cognac encouraged me to plan
ahead, to put off completing a project until it
had worked itself out or I felt the need to do
something at the moment. 1958 was to be the
crowning year with its burst of timely as well

as unlikely publications, with an aim at London,
as well as Lisbon and São Paulo. Ah, if only
the Gods had not so liked me as to deny me
my bit of pleasure at all the many *foguetes*
launched in singular tribute to me and mine.

May 14, 2013

Back to the Future

It would have fit—all of it—on one flash
drive. Imagine that, a single flash drive that
could easily be dropped into a pants pocket.
No need to save all that paper, worrying that
a small fire confined to one room—a bedroom
where there was the never occasional light-up
in bed—would burn all my work to a crisp,
for it would all be secure on the internet, riding
 or resting on the ever undulating air like one
of Hopkins's windhovers (or so I imagine).
Of course, there's the possibility too that one
of those early dump-pickers sniffing out the
espólio might just pocket the drive, thinking,
mistakenly, that he alone has got it entire.

May 15, 2013

The Line

Sometimes I think of it as an assembly line at its work,
those ambitious, curious, busy scholars who worked at
the papers, each one taking out the pieces (rather than
sticking something in as the "thing" goes by, though
that move is not entirely off the table either)—pieces
that can be assembled into a particular new whole. My
Aunt Lucy stuck the eyes in Mr. Potato Head—that was
her job—but, for all her wanting to do good, she never
cottoned to the figure or believed in its potential for play.

May 16, 2013

Sunday

It was always a tough day for me, the first day of the week,
mainly because I had to simulate an interest in my family,
sit down to breakfast with them, and leave off (they insisted,
if only silently) my interminable writing. And, of course,
the day's abstemiousness threw off my daily regimen of drink.
For posterity's sake, I even misdated some of my poems so as
to document that I had not neglected my writing, relegating it
to twenty-four/six as, of necessity, I had so done agreeably.
No unbuttoning my coat, hitching my belt, pushing my hat
back a bit rakishly, as I toss down a drink (see the Abel photo).
Day of rest? Day of abstinence. Loneliest day of the week.

May 19, 2013

Companions

I did not much like them, even less than my heteronyms.
Of course, Sá-Carneiro was something of an exception, but
even he, though dying young, had also tried my patience, as
anyone will see if they ever find my letters, which disappeared
along with his trunk, confiscated in lieu of his unpaid rent.
Álvaro de Campos was still around at the end (as has been
speculated), always a pain-in-the-ass to me, too, not just to
Ofélia or the editors of several journals. And as for Ricardo
Reis, when he sailed for Brazil, I could do no more than wish
him a cold bon voyage and a long stay (by which I meant a
permanent one). All that coterie ever did was make demands,
demands, demands. And of course, they were jealous of one
another, especially when I spent a moment working on
anything that did not involve them, and them alone.

May 20, 2013

Three Hundred

For better or worse,
without guile or *éclat*,
here's number three
hundred (actually 302),
written on somebody
or other's birthday.

May 23, 2013

What's for Breakfast?

There's a corner turned here, and
one more than half-expects to run
smack up against himself as he
walks through the morning *garoa*
down from the *Chiado* to the *Rua
Douradores* (if he is Bernardo) or
all the way down to the *Cais Sodré*
when the garb masks the other
cracker-jack-in-the-box jump-up.

May 29, 2013

Travel

No Saint Christopher medal for me,
for after I reached my maturity I went
nowhere, absolutely nowhere, if you

discount the trip up the coast to Cascais
for that librarian's job that I did not get
or the jaunt to Portalegre to buy all that

printing press paraphernalia that on balance
brought me nothing but misery. No, travel
was out for me, as it was for Caeiro and

Bernardo Soares. Álvaro, on the other hand,
was a sport in this (as in all things), and,
possibly to show me up, went everywhere,

even places, like the British Isles, that should
have appealed to me. How Ricardo Reis
managed to survive that relentless boat trip

to Brazil I'll never know. Come to think of it,
he never did write to me to let me know that
he had completed that escapist's voyage.

May 30, 2013

The Common Doom

That's what Henry James called it, though
the phrase was hardly original with him.
Nevertheless, it was in his writings that I
found it. What James meant by it, of course,
is that our impending death is something
we all share. But was that all he meant?
I think so. After all, when he sensed that
his own death was imminent, he is said to
have said "at last, the distinguished thing,"
or something along that line. He surely
did not mean that death was ordinary, banal,
i.e. common. Pessoa wrote down his last
words (or were they merely the last words
he wrote down?): *I know not what tomorrow
will bring.* Talk about your banalities.

May 31, 2013

Everyman (2)

Though not undervalued in his time,
now that he is dead everybody wants
a piece of him, or, more kindly, they
want a turn at the altar of praise.

There are pictures reeled in from drop-
box archives, old-line eulogies concocted,
and memories dredged up to amuse.
Would he have liked all this, or merely

condoned the effort? Oh, do not ask.
To paraphrase the novelist, the thing
about death is that it will make one
vulnerable, especially to easy praise.

June 2, 2013

Shoes, Socks, and Feet

Tonight I'm too tired to write the poem
I intended to write this morning. It was
to be something about socks and feet.

I thought I'd start with my memory of
Harold Larson, the truck mechanic of
more than sixty years ago, who always

slipped his feet into clean socks, first
one, then the other, before going home.
I was going to follow with a mention

of the freight solicitor, who borrowed
a pair of new socks from his boss and
did not return to work, scooting off to

California, never to be heard from again.
Pessoa would come next: the fact that
after Almada painted him sitting down

at a table, no one, except for the statue
in Cascais, ever saw him otherwise.
Witness the effigy outside *A Brasileira*.

I think to myself, wouldn't this man who
walked all over the Chiado and the Baixa,
down even, presumably, to the river, like

to stand and stretch a bit, maybe even walk
over to the deep stairs to the metro, take a
ride, see some of the drawings of himself

in one of the stations elsewhere on the line.
Then again, how much would he want to
walk if his shoes were as cement-heavy

as the ones standing him in good stead
in the Poet's Park? Of course, to resort
to a bad pun, it is bootless to so plant the

spruced-up walker-worker-poet. Should
we heed the U.S. Senator's advice to
change our shoes three, four times a day?

June 8, 2013

Staff of Life

Even the boy knew it, for he invented a
companion to talk to and then *O Palrador*,

which could make everything public, at
the least, to his self-determined readership.

What he was to determine, however, was
not only that he could not live by persons

alone but that there were *pessoas* even he
could not abide. So he killed some off and

let some of the others slide out of earshot,
caring not a whit for their commerce.

June 22, 2013

Parabens

At the Casa Fernando Pessoa, on the thirteenth of June,
there was a celebration of what would have been their
man's one-hundred-twenty-fifth birthday had he lived

so long and his sister had not thrown him out along the
way for drinking from his flask all night long, all the
while running up the electric bill (or the candle bill, his
choice). It is said that writers who have spent the night
in his room (we won't affirm that they have slept a wink)
have testified almost to a person that the spirit of the poet
is palpable. Doors open, doors close, sans human agency.
True or not, this is a good advertisement for a museum,
but not so good for your everyday bed-and-breakfast.

June 26, 2013

One Size Fits All

I always had the knack of convincing people, oblique
and obscure though my words might appear to be,
that I (and perhaps I alone) knew what I was talking
about. *Au contraire, mon cher.* I always counted on
others to make something out of the hodge-podge.

June 27, 2013

Now You Know

My taste has not soured, for it was never a factor or
a feature, nor has the salt lost its flavor. It took an
entire sea to get my attention and then only for the
time it takes to write a lyric laced with *saudade*.

June 30, 2013

242

Annoyance

Given the evidence of the writing that occupied me
that I left stretched out over all sorts of paper, literally
any scrap or letterhead that came to hand, you would
not think that in cafes I sometimes faked it—my mind
a total blank—so that those who should not disturb me
would not disturb me. It worked, for the most part, but
once in a great while some literate stranger from Porto
or Coimbra would stroll right up to where I was sitting
and interrupt my silence. No one who did that could
possibly have meant well, for they were aware that they
were interrupting me at my task, even when I was faking.
That fakery was something no one ever tumbled to.
Except, that is, Almada Negreiros. He was wise to me.
If you don't believe it, just look closely at the portrait
of me he painted for the Irmãos Unidos restaurant.

July 1, 2013

Statements

Most poems just do not get there.
In this, they are exactly like people.
*Statements made on the way
to the grave*, said the Welsh poet.
Sad to say, it's a precious few that
are worth making. Moreover, it's
a mug's game to pick among them.
By the way, what's to do when

a alma é pequena"? Answer me
that, Ramon Fernandez, you wag.

July 3, 2013

Honoris causa

Not in the cards for me, a non-native,
if honoured high-school graduate, one
exiled and trained in the schools of a
a distant British colony. I'm sure the
possibility of money never came up,
not then, not there, not anywhere.

July 3, 2013

Physiology

While the sonnet is friendly to the tragic
situations of *saudade*, the haiku is not,
for such spasms of feeling depend from
a fact: it is not that people suffer their
saudades (they do) but it is that destiny
decrees that they will suffer them time
and time again. If *a minha patria é a
minha língua, saudade* is its pathology.

July 4, 2013

Haiku (*à moda da casa*)

a minha pátria é
a minha língua e
o mal da saudade

July 6, 2013

To Each His Own

Ao que vos parece verso chamai verso, e
ao resto chamai prosa, said Irene Lisboa.
But I would say, *What strikes you as prose*
call prose; and what remains call poetry.

July 16, 2013

Have a Drink, Eat Some Cake, Live It Up

If they will celebrate the anniversary of the
formulation of the "intentional fallacy" (as
they did, in New Haven, some years back),
then why not throw a party on the putative
date of the putative birth of my heteronymic
project? No matter that it seems strange that
I never got around to writing up what I say
happened on that day until my very last year.
Caution though—I was ever the *blaguer*
(recall the message of *Mensagem*). So what
persuades anyone that I was offering straight

goods to the once highly overrated Adolfo
Casais Monteiro when I took up the gauntlet
and devised an answer to the questions asked
by that insistent pest? Of course, I knew it
was a doozy that would ring truer than truth.

July 17, 2013

Quem já não tem lua

Once upon a time the Iranian poets complained
that the Soviets, with their Luna-9 pictures of
its unappealing surface, had forever bitched the
moon for them. "'Now, with the ugly and coarse
surface' disclosed, Iranian poets must look for
something else to describe beauty,'" Ebrahim
Sahba said, speaking for the Iranian Poets Assoc.
Ah, the pity of it, the shelf-life semiotics of it all.

July 25, 2013

24/7

Damn that statue. It's a fate worse than death.
Death only makes one vulnerable, as Ralph's
mother says in *The Portrait of a Lady*. But
sitting there in the Chiado, near the long descent
to the metro station in the *Baixa* brings to mind
the fate of the near-stationary Wal-Mart greeter.
(That's a wild anachronism, I know, but I can't

resist making the so-apt comparison, especially
since it was always a hallmark of mine to make
every effort to keep up-to-date.) Of course, I
do sit in a chair, but, like Tantalus, I'm fixed.

July 27, 2013

Distich

If *recordar é viver*
(*vox populi*), then
viver é also *recordar*
(not *vox populi*).

Aug. 9, 2013

Soon

There comes a day when the world knows you no more.
It will soon forget you, but the act of forgetting never
begins from scratch. It has had a long logic behind it,
for forgetting will always begin in plenty of time, just so
that all is just so for the crescendo when the end comes
and the watchers of the dead devolve and wane.

Aug. 9, 2013

Álvaro in Nighttown

Cruising the Cais de Sodré
where no showgirl donned a
pasty and the *pastéis de Belém*
were not yet all the rage, he
queried his tactics but never
his motives. And so his life
dragged on, a conquest here,
a failure there, *unsoweiter*.

Aug. 10, 2013

A Conceit

It's as if each heteronym was a
specialized self-storage unit, a
warehouse, if you will, for his
varied and contrarian thoughts.
Some of these lockers he filled
beyond their capacity, others he
left half-filled, and still others
he abandoned with little or
nothing in them. His followers
mostly play at storage wars, a
game in which each of them
has paid nothing to look into a
black box jammed with ciphers.

Aug. 10, 2013

Do Not Ask

The New York *Times* keeps a daily list
of the "notable deaths of the year," but
all deaths, I would say, are notable even
if the New York *Times* doesn't take note
of them. The vanity of human wishes
does not know *notable* from *noticed.*

Aug. 12, 2013

Malgré lui

Adolfo Rocha did not like what
Fernando Pessoa said about his
poetry so he became Miguel
Torga to show the Master that
Alberto Caeiro was not the only
one who could do the pastoral
thing. And from that moment
he sought out no one's stamp.

Aug. 12, 2013

Apres vous

Having looked down on the marvels
of the earth through the lens of a camera

moving about in space, he found that he
no longer looked up in awe or abandon.

Aug. 14, 2013

Posterity's Revenge

I'm willful, argumentative, and unpleasant,
but I keep all this pretty much to myself.
It makes for much writing that I can stock-
pile and warehouse until I have a block or
two of disposable time when I will revise
and tame it all to some semblance of order.
Fat chance, I know, since all this writing
and revising amounts to nothing more, as
the Brits will tell you, than a mug's game.

Aug. 17, 2013

The Choice

William Butler Yeats, the Willie
who traded on his patrician lineage
even as he espoused the cause of
the oppressed Irish, proclaimed that
to achieve perfection a poet must
choose between the life and the work.
Patronizing, as was his wont, he never
quite saw what the God-fearing chaps
all around him had had the moxie to

try to do, After all, it's pretty to think
the choice has legs, though life, going
along with the sham, does as it will.
Ask Joyce, ask Pessoa, ask Marcel.

Aug. 18, 2013

No Title

It was Jorge de Sena who noticed that the title one gives one's
poem constitutes a second poem. He said so in a poem that
was not one of his so-called criticism-poems (he tried out that
idea in prose) but what one may call a literary theory-poem.
Yet not quite buying the concept, the Master (*avant la lettre*, of
course) was as often as not too much the procrastinator (wily,
timid—your choice) to settle on titles. After all, there's a time
to revise, a time to re-title, as the Preacher might have written.
But as my good aunt so often noted, *o tempo só falta no fim.*

Aug. 21, 2013

Stones

No one who saw him walking the *calçado do Chiado*
could tell that he walked with a stone in his shoe, one
larger than Lisbon, larger than the earth, and, yes,
larger even than the galaxy of galaxies. In thought,
of course, he ranged as widely and deeply as his brain
chose to ride him, but sooner rather than later he came
back down to History—the history of his fellow *lusiadas*

and their diminished present situation, that is, their sorry
plight as figured in his time. There was a stone in their
way, one that could not be rolled away or, for that matter,
evaded. Historical literalists called it Sebastian, abstracted
ambiguously, in time, into the maladies of *Sebastianismo*,
pretending that it had (has) the reality of a thing among
things. Even he couldn't work his people into taking
advantage of a myth that was everything, and nothing.

Aug. 22, 2013

O Além

I've never believed in the beyond
but then I have never disbelieved
in it either. It's never been much
of a factor in my thinking or my
being. Death I think about a lot
and have always been sensitive
to its hovering presence. Heming-
way was once accused of being
fixed in adolescence because he
could not come to terms with the
fact of death and thus put it behind
him. I wondered at that, not Hem's
obsession with death (I shared that)
but whether his critic was in the right.
It took me years to put the critic's

words behind me (his name not)—
a victory that failed to please me.

Aug. 23, 2013

Engels's Dog

Alerted to the presence
in the café of the hated
by the cry *Aristocrat!*
Friedrich Engels's dog
would snap to the pose
and bark like nobody's
business. So legend has
it. But I say it is not a
legend because, let's
face it, this *is* a dog's
world or, to be fair in
this, it should be.

Aug. 23, 2013

Not His Problem

He must have written about the moon
but offhand I can't think of an instance
when he did. It is said when space
cameras brought us close-up shots of its
unimpressive surface, unshapely with
unfamiliar and unfriendly contours,

Iranian poets to a man let out a howl
that this new knowledge deprived them
of their symbol par excellence for
beauty. New knowledge is like that.

Aug. 27, 2013

I Say

no one but no one
can write like Pessoa,
least of all himself.
Just show me if you
can the man who
can put up a good
fight against the
legend he has built
for himself.

Aug. 27, 2013

Death in Paris

It took me a long time to swallow the hard truth
that my friendship had not been enough to keep
him rooted to this earthly place for his allotted
three score and ten. But it hadn't been enough,
and my guilt and regret emerged at the strangest
and unexpected moments, when I happened to be
in the vicinity as the periodic train from Paris eased

nosily into the Rossio station. Even Sidónio's death
in that self-same place brought me only the cold
comfort that at least you had assassinated yourself.

Aug. 28, 2013

Bright Idea

Anyone can write a book, if one
has opinions, and keeps notes.

Oct. 5, 2013

No Egg, No Columbus

He was a Zelig of ideas and sentiments,
always around when something of the sort
came up, though none of them, speaking
strictly, was of his devising or, if truth be
known, held on to for long. Thesis and
antithesis, yes. Synthesis? Not so much.

Oct. 6, 2013

Day Work

It suited him fine, this jobber's job,
and he dressed accordingly, calling
in every day to see if there was some

thing or other he could help with. As
such, he could fructify the fiction that
he was his own man, self-employed,
entrepreneurial, not required to punch
a clock, not pinned to a desk or a type-
writer until dinner-time. Pity that he
had no other income, though, for most
of the time at least, since it was true
that Álvaro had gone off to Portalegre
to spend his (not Álvaro's) wherewithal—
a modest inheritance—on a press he had
hauled back to Lisbon to ensure his (not
Álvaro's) failure at the printer's trade.

Oct. 6, 2013

Colleagues at 100, at 125

T. S. Eliot was 25 when Vinicius was born, which
makes Vinicius a late or second-generation modernist.
Who would you rather praise, the querulous Sybil of
The Waste Land or the burly enunciator of the refrain
Hoje é sábado? The progenitor of Prufrock's self-
sorrow or the seaside *chope* drinker who bleats out his
complaint? This is a not a test. But it is a no-brainer.

Oct. 14, 2013

Climate Change

It has everything to do with the weather,
but not today, this week or this year.
Imagining his last morning, Caeiro cast
himself as the sun's salutatorian.
Ricardo always lived darkly as if he were
under a great cloud. Good or bad, the
weather never suited Campos, who day-in,
day-out, with the mien of a man of purpose,
would once in a great while look about
and complain (but not for long, though,
so busy was he turning the world into his
own affair). Bernardo sat at his desk all
morning and knew rain only when he
stepped outside to get his *almoço*. Mora
wondered why his hat was wet when he
took it off in the vestibule. Now Botto
sang and danced in the rain (his fedora
told the story), while Almada recognized
inclemency if it suited him to do so.
As for *ele-mesmo*, he never failed to
record the minutest change overhead
as proof that the pathetic fallacy rules.

Oct. 25, 2013

Blame

Solipsist that I was, I always took
on the blame myself. It never
crossed my mind to share it with
anyone else. Álvaro approved.
No blame games for me, no. My
sport was *charadas*. (Truth told
though, it was all sport—all of it.)

Oct. 29, 2013

Slip the Yoke

Archly, he said that he experienced *saudades*
not for those as he had once known them but
for them as the survivors they would now be.

Oct. 29, 2013

Faux amis

Ordinary / *ordinário* is the example
for today. The former is descriptive,
denotative. The latter is denotative, but
description is judgmental, dismissive,
condemnatory. The one encourages you
to look at things at the level of level, eye
to eye; the other, to look down on a person
who if he weren't such an *ordinário* to

begin with, would cast down his eyes in
abject shame. It's what a *faux ami* will do.

Oct. 29, 2013

Repurposing

The words of the dead are
modified in the guts of the
living (or some such twaddle),
wrote the living poet elegizing
the just-then-dead Yeats. If
so, such deviant appropriation
comes natural to the species.

Oct. 29, 2013

Sixes and Sevens

He who outgrows his size
before outgrowing his dress,
lives the life that shows you
things are out of joint. It is
not the economy that's to
blame. No, not Hamlet, not
Horatio. It *is* the stars.

Oct. 31, 2013

The Day Between

It is not reported that he took along
something to read before sleeping
this last night in the hospital, though
he did have access to paper and some-

thing to write with. We know this
because he left behind a one-sentence
note, words that made clear sense to
himself, but were cryptic to everyone

else. Come to think of it, the paper,
the pencil, were his own, resting there,
as ever in the pocket of his everyday
paletot (a Brazilian term won't hurt

credibility, will it?), close to hand for
setting down a note between assignments
or, perhaps, when drinking at Abel's.
When did he know that he would not

make it through the night? When did
he realize that he had made a mistake
when casting his own horoscope months
before, and the early death presaged did

not happen, thus increasing his portion.
The error had relaxed him such, that right
off he was able to concoct his myth
describing the rise to consciousness of

his most famous heteronyms—a fabulation
that the sniffing Adolfo swallowed hook,
line, and sinker—as well as poems about
the mediocrity of the politico who shared

his Christian middle name but precious little
else. In any case, his illness had worsened
quickly that afternoon such that in a flash
his doctor (or someone else) had him

whisked away to the French hospital. He
was to be treated by the family's doctor,
so termed, not only because he treated the
whole family but because he was also a

member of the family. Maybe this doctor
wasn't the best of doctors (or even a good
one), the poet may have wondered, as his
whole system seemed patently determined

to shut down, wondering, moreover (though
it was too late now), if he should have
placed himself in the hands of one more
competent, more alert to symptoms,

than was this doctor-in-and-of-the-family.
In Durban, the family doctor was felt to be
top-notch—father to Roy Campbell, the
poet, who later claimed to have sat at the

same school desk on which the Portuguese
child had carved his name. All this, in some

hidden way, was part of the back story to
the words the dying poet left behind on that

piece of paper on his hospital bedside stand,
words meant for himself or (as it turned out)
posterity. And, of course, since the next
day was a Sunday, he could rest up (in his

own writer's fashion) and be back at work
composing commercial letters on Monday.
Better he had fallen ill on a weekday and
missed a day or two of writing those business

letters for those firms that were too busy
getting on, sometimes, to actually get on.
Or was all the subsequent speculation as
to what it all meant wildly misguided and

sadly mistaken? That he, adventurer of the
imaginary that he was, was really looking
forward to a new day with its necessarily
modified living circumstances? The chance

that being a professionally cared-for ordinary
patient would be refreshing? Leisure, a rare
(really absent) commodity in his life, though
it was something his friends and acquaintance,

who knew nothing of the hours and days he
spent writing at the tall chest of drawers in his
room, his door closed, would have recognized
as the lack in his life. In all probability, some

thought that the *cruz na porta* this time would
refer to his corpse must have crossed his mind as
he lay there, as everything that mattered to him
—light, work, life—closed down around him.

Did he think of the goodbyes that he had failed
to say? Did he trifle away his moments in such
bootless reveries? What, no antithesis to this
thesis? Or was this already the synthesis of

thought that he set down on paper? Would
the newspapers notice? Would the *Times*,
London or New York? And what, by the way,
was it that was taking him off? Nothing poetic,

like Keats's consumption, or Chekhov's, but
cirrhosis, the plain old drinker's common curse.
And too late now, but he did wish that he'd had
another year, six months, or even just a few

long days (imminence would then have a date)
to revise, to cull and arrange the depressive
Bernardo's *pensées* (that's too grandiose, too
honorific a category, surely, for those jottings,

that marginalia), gathered to justify a catch-all
(loosely unifying) title that just wouldn't do.
Now, of course, he did feel a modicum of—
confess it—uncharacteristic regret, for all those

now bootless tasks. But then, losing it all would
not be all that bad. Maybe not—though, to be sure,

he hadn't gotten close to that painter's grasp, not
even, sadly, his reach. The question, as he now saw

it, was not exactly the one postulated by the Bard's
poseur, but rather when (if ever) does jealousy
cease once and for all. His jealousy—think now
Ophelia, think Álvaro (no saints there)—only a

silence, reminding us that there is no recording
of his many voices, no way to know what sounds
he made when he spoke, when he sang, if he sang,
or when he cackled back at the *galego*'s raven.

Nov. 1 / 6, 2013

That's It?

The desire,
a wish, and
memory.

Nov. 6, 2013

Doing the Ibis

For a long time he took it as clear evidence
that he could hold his liquor. Amusing the
young by striking the pose of the awkward
ibis, he took to doing it silently when alone
in his room after a night of steady drinking.

Then he couldn't do it anymore. It was then
he knew he had a problem. It didn't stop him,
though losing his one sure talent was sobering.

Nov. 17, 2013

Loyalty

He was always loyal to friends,
Botto, Almada, Antonio Ferro,

even Raul Leal, so long as they
didn't get too close. Never did

he burn so happily for anyone
else as he did for Sá-Carneiro

when his spiritual other took his
Luso act to Parisian venues.

Barkeeps and all merchants of
drink, though, were pre-approved.

Nov. 21, 2013

The Purlieus

We met at the Martinho for many reasons, I guess,
beyond those that called for drinking and snacking,
or the fact that the management recognized that we

required a table reserved for the self-chosen cabal
that we thought we were. Privately, though, I saw
the leaving of it each time, stepping through the
doorway, the Terreiro do Paço reaching out to the
Tejo and expanding before us into clear or, rarely,
clouded skies—all that, as a momentary stay against
the habit of my daily confusions. Then to beat a path
to the homely noise and shocks of my nocturnal life.

Nov. 22, 2013

Work *and* Life?

A circumspect biographer of the Anglo-American writer
Henry James writes: *To link work with life is plausible
only in the knowledge that a writer will transmute actuality
into something else.* I think I agree with this, but only as
far as it goes, for do we not need to say more, may I add,
about what, in its particulars, actually makes up *actuality*?

Nov. 22, 2013

The Chocolates

Ginsberg imagined Whitman,
awe-struck at a California super-
market, wanting to know who killed
the pork chops. Which, of course,
reminds me. In the poem in which
Campos famously advises a child

in the street to eat away at her
chocolates, an act of metaphysics,
how did she come by her chocolates?
Any answer, surely, is obvious.

Nov. 23, 2013

One Down

In 1906, when he was 18, he set down
the name of one fictitious being few
readers have seen as one of his other
identities—*Ferdinand Sumwan*—one
that the young poet went on to explain
(as if he needed to make it real to him-
self): *Fernando Pessoa, since Sum=
Some One=Person=Pessoa)*. To boot,
he was (or was deemed to be, as the poet
saw him) *a normal, useless, lazy, careless,
weak individual*. Of course, nothing
more came of this *Ferdinand Sumwan*,
for who could have envisioned him as
having the gumption to stir himself to
write something of value or, truth be told,
anything at all. It was never in the cards.

Nov. 26, 2013

History

The Brits fancy Jacks, the Portingales, Damas.
Queen Elizabeth was a Brit, Dom Sebastião, a

Portingale. Yet it might have worked out to
great avail had these royalties been swapped.

The Portuguese would not have lost as many
ships, though the world's seven seas would

be famished for tears. And the Brits, they
might have soldiered away until the planet

was civilized to the last of its purlieus. If
the past harbors a horse, it scorns a wish.

Nov. 29, 2013

He Didn't Get It in 1935

I tell you he didn't get the big one.
That year no one won it. *Wait 'till*

next year, that's the ticket
—expect stones, not bread.

Nov. 30, 2013

Pride of Place

It was assigned to Himself
at the first dinner, arranged by
the engineer for a mere five;

he was set up at the head of
the round table, rather like the
defunct Jeremy at one of those

rare meetings of the Council,
where he was noted as "present
but not voting." The engineer's

rule was that Himself was not
to open his mouth, not if queried
or provoked. The others, though,

could hold forth, politely or not.
It was hard at first for the fêted
guest to hold his peace, so he bit

his tongue, and schemed revenge:
an early death, exile abroad, a
dead-end job, and *aldravice*.

Dec. 9, 2013

Por ele-mesmo

Poems about the birth of Jesus,
poems dedicated to the saints
closest to the popular bosom
but not a word for Guy Fawkes.

Dec. 10, 2013

Horizons Are

the imaginary's strip-tease caught in a loop,
the sailor's hope that there is something out there,
the weary sojourner's last recourse (if he can only get there),
the lover's surety that love is in the offing while fearing that it
will always be so, the stubborn knight's hope against despair,
flung like a handful of sand into the wind, and the mists
that do not bring forth the promised savior, and the mists
that do not bring forth the savior.

Dec. 14, 2013

Oh No

When I realized that now, for the first time,
I was older than the reigning Pope, and Him-
self no spring chicken, I thought it time to
get cracking, though, I'm afraid, it's too late.

Dec. 17, 2013

Esquilo

Centuries, it seems, since this
squirrel stood up, showing off
his nuts, as he hath told us—
with a few facts a bit askew.
But his play was a good one,
and, for a time, it stuck.

Jan. 11, 2014

Fim de contas

Ricardo Reis, excruciating, devoid of human sympathies
except for himself.
Alberto Caeiro, a cistern in which to empty all the attention
that Nature is due.
Bernardo Soares, a Bartleby with no self-knowledge.
Antonio Mora, a sententious player in the kindergarten of
thought.
Álvaro de Campos, a blamer, and, by turns, a loud complainer,
Alexander Search and C. R. Anon, feckless, non-survivors.
Chevalier de Pas, needful, for the moment.

Jan. 18, 2014

Prince Hal

slipped Pessoa into his
pantheon of 26 (so few,

so many), paragons
of a Western canon.
How altruistic, it
might be opined,
of the assiduous
king, the decider.

Jan. 29, 2014

Consilience

The dream that it is
all we will ever know
is not popular with
the populace at large.

Feb. 8, 2014

Even Poets

must die, for
how else can
their words
be so wrenched
as to achieve
other meanings
in the guts
of the living
or the decks,
so to speak.

be cleared
to prepare
for the second,
for the third,
for the next
coming?

Feb. 8, 2014

Not Knowledge, Not Awe

What they say about cancer,
that more people live off
the disease than die from it,
is also true about my leavings,
my scraps—pills, bitter to
swallow, but sweet, too.

Feb. 13, 2014

Fragment

He was no patron at the shop of fragments.
His hubris was that he would live long enough
and die well enough to finish, at some point or
other, everything that he had had to leave
unfinished. Even life itself was to him but a
fragment he never did come to terms with,

let alone accept as it was, always looking
forward to what tomorrow might bring.

Feb. 18, 2014

Lesson for Today

Poetry always wants to be more than it is.
Its megalomania knows no bounds.

Poets, on the other hand, are relieved
to have finished a poem—or should be.

Feb. 21, 2014

Acordo ortográfico

Without a second thought (as far as we know),
he took the direct, major action (as he described
it) of dropping the diacritical mark riding herd
over his patronym, explaining that the move
would buckle him closer to an English-reading
public. It did not help, not one scintilla's worth.

Feb. 22, 2014

Vox populi

The poetry was never intended to speak to
the populace or be in any way the voice
of the people. Yet neither were the words
to be the words of poesy though they were
intended in their arranged aggregate to make
poetry. The poems were to sound demotic
without being themselves demotic. There
was nothing natural in the making of what,
at their best, passed for natural works. It was
a tricky business always, and in the unfinished
poems he left spaces for words to be supplied
later when out of the blue the better word would
come to him and beg to be slipped into place.

Mar.1, 2014

No Ashes

Wrote Álvaro de Campos:
quanto fui, quanto não fui,
tudo isso sou. Easy for him
to say, he who never wrote
anybody's bio (and a good
thing, too, since his sneers
and habitual snark was the
cause of not wit in others
but withdrawal into the self).
Yet, in another sense, this
obnoxious performer of a

public self has been nothing
but catnip to legions of awe.

Mar. 5, 2014

Sleepy Time

They will write of the experience of having slept
one night in the poet's last room at his sister's
house and, along with other such pieces, it will go
into a book. This venture, to my mind, is based
on the shaky premise that Himself actually slept
when there. Yet, somehow I find it hard to believe
that he did sleep in that room. I'm thinking that
he was an insomniac, standing tall (all of 5' 6")
at the chest, writing away and dropping scrawl
after scrawl to the floor around him. Sleep? He
did that at the offices of Dupin and others in the
Baixa. I've been in that room myself and had a
sensation that there was still the occasional scrap
of paper floating down from the chest to the floor.

Mar. 5, 2014

Selfies

Novelty, popularity, and fashion
being what they are, coming and

going and coming and going as
is the wont of some, and before

it goes the way of the dodo bird,
I thought it best to get this down.

On face-book a young *pessoana*
posts a selfie of herself and the

Eduardo Lourenço de Faria over
the legend that he so much loved

having the act and the product
explained to him. Think back

now to what it might have meant
to Himself had a device such

as this been around on that day
in 1914. O.K., these poets have
sprung up, not like Athena from
the head of Zeus (proven by a

selfie or two that we won't trust),
but from Almada's head or heart.

Mar. 6, 2014

To Be is to Be Different

I could not travel and be myself, not even in fantasy.
I could not be different by myself and therefore be.
It was no malady that afflicted me, only a quirk of
consciousness and thus not be questioned by me or
treated by any of those whose calling is to treat. It
was not original to me but it was in my very bones.

Mar. 7, 2014

Fate

Always somebody else's bucket list,
their bottomless cup.

Mar. 8, 2014

A Poet's Query

*Mas porque será sempre 'Lídia,' a
pegar nas rosas, Dr. Ricardo Reis?*
Who knows for sure? But try this
one on, if you will: the kooky doc
was role-playing the saintly queen,
once again nailing down her brazen,
outrageous lie to a nosy, kinky king.

Mar. 8, 2014

Catch My Drift

O.K. So it was one Zeus,
and one Athena. But stick
with me, for there's smoke
here. Imagine, three poets
popping from the one head,
the head of one in need,
one who, ten years down the
line, gave birth to an *Athena*.

Mar. 9, 2014

Poet, Frequent Flyer

Thinking I might improve
the day on this two-hour
flight or at least occupy
myself at something to
help me pass this other-
wise personal white-out
time, not wanting to read
(besides I have no book
along) or to strike up a
conversation with a
stranger at my side or
across the aisle, I think:
write a poem, brushing
aside the useful warning
the world needs no more

poems, at least not from
me, for a man's grasp
will never exceed his
reach; nor is it always
wise to reach at all,
even if one is bored
stiff, bored to tears.
Old habits never die;
they just self-justify.

Mar. 24, 2014

Cash Cow

"The greatest book ever written,"
writes an obviously over-heated
blogger. But Sontag and Steiner
were only slightly behind this
boast in their extravagant praise
for this post-modernist's wet dream
of a " book" the author not only
never wrote to the finish but didn't
leave the slightest hint as to his
wish for a final design, structure,
shape, let alone a working plan for
experimenting with the arrangement
of these meanderings, more often than
not kvetches, of a low-level bookkeeper.
But today's reader loves the fragment;
it makes everything so tentative, so
indefinite, so all everything's-in-the-

offing. So we select and arrange,
pick and print: thus the newest best
text appears with the passing of each
new season. *Pano pra manga* for
the reader who has time, itch, scratch
and inclination to sup on what every-
day authorial posterity will dish up.
Next up, on the list at last, is the *livro
de bolso*, courtesy of *tinta-da-china*.

Apr. 4, 2014

Self-knowing

 "I only eat so I can smoke
and stay alive," says Repo
man, while another says,
sotto voce, "I stay alive so
I can eat." Note the gamut.

Apr. 8, 2014

Such Poems

Some say the good poem will turn to
ire. Some say it must flicker into fire.
But from what I know of all this, fire

and ire are more than a poem of this
sort requires for its versy denouement.

Apr, 13, 2014

The Earth Did Not Shake

In 1616, on this day, in this month,
at home, in Stratford-on-Avon, died
the person who answered to 'William
Shakespeare," still rich in corn, but
done with playing, having left not a
word unsaid or one favor uncurried.

Apr. 23, 2014

The Truth Is Not in Him

He told lies, of course; in that
he was no different from you
or me. But he differed from
us in that he was far more adept
at getting others to buy in when
they should have known better.
Take his lie to his friend Almada
that it was drink that made him
say those mean things about his
drawings that he did not mean.
Or the Boca do Inferno murder
of Aleister Crowley, a tissue of

misinformation that has not yet
sifted down to one truth. The
corker, though, is the big lie in
the screed to the gullible Casais,
Monteiro, who bought into that
foundational myth, hook, line,
and sinker—as we all do.

May 7, 2014

The Wit of One

To keep love pure don't mix
it with experience. If you
want to express something,
don't blurt out its name.
For example, take the word
saudade… Take it, please.

June 5, 2014

Tremoços & Sagres

Had they feasted
on such a diet,
they would never
have gotten there.
But wait, they did
not get *there*, did
they? Only later

did they so pertly
retell a sober tale.

June 13, 2014

História

It's always our last recourse, as well as our first,
and there's nothing else to tide us over. It is the
appeal, the argument, the justification, and, in a
pinch, the tragedy overall. We are because we
were, and we shall be for the same steadfast reason.
Tell it to the stars, tell it to the marines, tell it to
the sticks and stones even. It will not matter.
The story has brought us this far, and while it may
not bear looking into, it is our meat, our drink.

June 16, 2014

Apotheosis

My likeness is stamped on a cookie. What can
be next, for god's sake! Face on a potato chip?
Effigy showing forth from a singular evergreen
cracked wide by the accuracy of a lightning bolt?
Etch a-sketch transforming the back of a luckless
shepherd as he prays against the mercy of rain?

July 7, 2014

Signage

There simply aren't enough plaques. Not nearly
enough to mark out the walks of my days, the
meanderings of a holiday. Maybe that's a good
thing, given my habitual peripathy. There was
no metro in my day, and I didn't much take to
the trolley. Getting there was seldom a worry.
Still, a sign or two more wouldn't hurt, huh?

July 8, 2014

The Book

The luck in this case lay in advertising this book by
title, as the work of others, that book I did not come
close to shaping up. Jorge de Sena saw the chance
for a selection of these bits in dishabille if ordered,
but he did not go beyond advertising his intentions.
So when Maria Aliete Galhoz and Teresa Sobral
Cunha did the job, their honest work was farmed
out to Jacinto do Prado Coelho, considered by the
knowing at the time to be *perito* in the matter, who
methodically laid out a book that enjoyed a modest
success. Jump ahead a few years. Various hands,
 in turn, take up the task anew, and make it, kit and
caboodle, a kaleidoscope with determinants to be set
at will, giving this book that never was a sterling place

among the century's best. Only in Portugal, some
will say, though not I.

July 8, 2014

The Time of Its Time

Time and again he left for tomorrow
what he could have done that day.
The result was that though he marked
many of the notes and aperçus, as to the
literary destination of the accumulation
as a whole, he left that, to put it kindly,
in dishabille. Who touched those pieces
first, who first meddled with them, that
remains hidden. But at some point it
was decided to keep track of them by
numbering them in accordance with
some crude system that gradually lost
its determinant sway. So, within limits,
it was all up for grabs. And grab they
did, such that the "book" has become
a model for literary modernism. No
Leaves of Grass, the *Livro* has its own
aspects, changing as light will change,
meaning all things or nothing to those
who see it as a passel of fragments
embodying whatever semblance of
authorial intention a fragment can offer.
It rides the wave, this last, unfinished

masterpiece by, indisputably, a master.
Yes, it rides the crest of the big wave.

July 9, 2014

Taking to the Road

When the *sucatas* in Britain dried up, his
own byronic hero, blessed with the best
alien training (Glasgow), returned to Lisbon,
jobless and broke, desperate now to drive
a borrowed Chevrolet over the road to
Sintra, chasing work, rumors of work.

July 10, 2014

Not Your Grandmother's *Copa*

Give me a resounding defeat anytime
over an expected and well-deserved
victory. The debacle at the hands of
a workmanlike German team (as good
but no better than one might expect
of an appetitive nation) inspires such
spillage of words and jokes that outs
the outdoor Copacabana mass at the
outset of the sixteenth-century (or the
fifteenth, if we go by a Lusitanian

count) as somewhat less than a blip
in the vaunted annals of the place.

July 12, 2014

A Plan

The folk have a little rhyme,
a rhyme that tells it all.

> *À morte ninguém escapa.*
> *Nem o rei, nem o duque,*
> *nem o papa. Mas ca eu*
> *eide escapar. Compro uma*
> *panela, custa-me um vintém,*
> *meto-me dentro dela e tapo-*
> *a muito bem. E quando a*
> *morte passa, ela diz: 'aqui*
> *não mora ninguém,' e passa.*
> *E quando está la longe, digo*
> *eu, 'passa, passa muito bem.'*

And then, soon enough, there
were none, none to speak up.

July 29, 2014

A Note on the Sublime

You know you're in trouble,
deep do-do, when you find
The Ruin more moving, more
captivating than the original
would have struck you in
its day. But 'so what?' you
shrug. And you're right.
he very existence of an
old *baú* makes its point.

Sept. 2, 2014

O balanço

After all the books, the conferences,
the somber attention of universities
in cities all across the map, can we
not say, at the last, that the life, brutal
and short, was worth it? *Pois não, há
ainda quem diz que nada deu certo
nessa vida em que nada deu certo.*

Sept. 19, 2014

Sir Francis Bacon

He, who took all knowledge to be his province,
who, a jurist, rendered honest, judicious verdicts
(but took bribes), and, who, an ever practical man,
died from complications linked to riding in a cab
with a chicken in an experiment in refrigeration,
an experiment tried, of course, after he had written
every one of Shakespeare's words—it is no wonder
he caught the intense attention of one who gave up
love and marriage hands down for the sake of his
"work" (so he said), one who had no interest in
refrigeration (as far as we know), but did risk it all
on a single throw, a single casting of the horoscope.

Sept. 21, 2014

Surmising

"Start to be a *mensch*"—the sort of command
alien to himself, he who asked Antonio Botto
(it's verified) to call him *menino* and to treat
him accordingly. *Tem juizo, Fernando!*—
words never far from the lips of the Consul.

Sept. 29, 2014

Not Quite Right

Cross-stitched, two thoughts come to mind:
when depressed I could not write except in
the *Desassossego*, and the other? 'most men
lead lives of quiet desperation.' Bartleby?

Oct. 12, 2014

Blessed Be

the working poet who works out the lines, and blessed be
the distracted crow that dusts down snow, saving the day

of the man that rues. And blessed, too, be the *galego* crow,
back-talking to the drinker hiding his hand in his pocket.

Fame

> I live in my work—a poet in my poems *really*—
> but only curiously after my death—
>   Pessoa (1911-13)

Would he have been numbered among the greats, like
John Keats, Blake, the chosen few others? The Fates
know, but they don't talk, at least haven't until now. The
English world, however (*pace* the first responders or self-
proclaimed pundits), has ingested the gist of it by way of
the no longer small horde of translators who have carried
water for him, for his leavings. Then there's this. There

are those many who see it all as a just compensation for
the loss of what was not meant to be, a metaphoric heritage
of waters that otherwise would never have floated a sailor.

Feb. 11, 2015

Orpheu, for Starters

It played bigger than its deserts
but smaller than the scheme.

O poeta é um fingidor; yet
the poet does not lie, for he

asserts nothing. Make it new,
demands the American, then

permits himself to live a life
enumerating the (boring) past.

In Cascais, he learns that to
be over-qualified is also to be

under-qualified. Inventive to a
fault, he bows only to Edison.

It is not with Mardi Gras in
mind that he talks up the mask.

Unemployed since the discovery of
India, he locks himself into History.

Set loose, his personae take over
the drama, finagling for command.

He who repeats himself does not
contradict himself. His poet friend

in Paris takes to strychnine—once
—as the peregrine falcon rides air

over a sea churning into whitecaps,
a sea spilling over whitecaps.

Feb. 17, 2015

Derby Time

Making the weight is not in question
when the choice is made as to who
will next ride that human Citation.
The steed, a comet, its tail on fire,
performs the trick of never flaming
out of sight. Still the rider, the same
one of late, does his due diligence
and thus his duty; and the winner of
this one-horse challenge stays true.

Feb. 23, 2015

Apologia pro vita sua

Whenever I rolled up my sleeves
it was not to get down to work or
to stick a needle in my arm but to

keep my shirt from getting wet
while I shaved or washed my face.
You cannot live in God, said Roshi

to Leonard, *There are no restaurants
or toilets there*. As for closets, advised
Elizabeth Bishop, you can never have

enough of them, and she wasn't talking
about living in God. For all the good he's
said to have done, my lasting memory

of the famous poet is that of a sure-footed,
slow-walking thief making off with a
a couple of bottles of wine—dago red—

stolen from the table at the out-of-doors
lunch at a small-potatoes Lisbon conference.
"Let it go," advised the one in charge.

They did, and the rascal kept on walking
to the bus and into the shade of its insides.
Like the German statesman who in his

80s planted apple seedlings for his
grandsons to enjoy in the far-off future,
so, too, did the unemployable poet do

his work for the future, for grandsons
he would not have or would have liked.
Now that we know that drummers' brains

are different from all others, what a pity
no one in the entourage took up sticks.
Out of the window of a small hotel in

Montreal I have seen a bird (no, birds)
on a wire screen and learned how a word
and a melody can falsify things as they

otherwise are. Looking ain't seeing,
or is it, that seeing needs no looking.
He liked a clean collar (who wouldn't?)

and a freshly pressed suit, always wanting
to leave a good impression among those
who noticed him as he walked the Chiado

of a weekday or Sunday. That's who he was.
Ah, the fate of the disabled man to become
a Wal-Mart greeter, not unlike a figure cast

in bronze, shilling for the drinking hole at
his back. Even a paranoid has friends; he
called them heteronyms. He reached out

295

to English, the language of necessity if
not choice; but, ignored, he fell back on
Portuguese. Mirandês? *Nem pensar.*

Feb. 24 / Mar. 1, 2015

Antonio Ferro, *Orpheu* and Beyond

In 2015, a cool one hundred years
after the publication of the first issue

of *Orpheu*, a journal which, in its 2
issues, scandalized pretty much all

of Portugal, there are conferences
lined up in Portugal and Brazil, as

well as exhibitions mounted in the
same cities. There is even one at

the Library of Congress in the U. S.
of A. (though nothing is planned,

as far as I know, for London or, for
that matter, Durban). Time has

long since confined itself to singling
out for our attention figures such as

Mário de Sá-Carneiro, Almada
Negreiros, and, of course, Pessoa.

Seldom acknowledged, though (and
then only grudgingly), is the role of

Ferro (money, yes, but no literary
contributions from this baby in the

putsch). Undoubtedly, his years
afterwards as a risk-taking news-

man (conducting sympathetic
interviews with fascist heads-of-

state) or as the eager-beaver, self-
promoting publicist of Salazar's

thumb-screws rule. But forgot
is his unflagging loyalty to a

Modernist agenda, promoting the
literature, architecture, and lore

of his country. Re-open the case.
The stakes are justice, fairness

Mar. 8, 2015

The Trio Mark

Prudence called for internment,
so the poet was given a bed at

the hospital of the doctor's choice.
The poet asked that paper and

pencil be set out at his side, sure
enough that he would need them

(as he always did) to glean his
teeming brain. But his Muse

said nothing, kicking him, so to
speak, to the curb, with not even

the common courtesy of a shout-
out—one like, say, *Nevermore!*

Mar. 10, 2015

Obsequies

His passing was duly noted in all the journals
(though later, to further the myth, it was claimed
otherwise). The usual suspects were at the church
—Almada, Antonio Ferro, Casais Monteiro (I think)
—but not Ophelia (her presence would have seemed
unseemly). Her nephew Carlos Queiros was there,
planning his radio broadcast tribute, as well as Gaspar

Simões, laying out in his mind what should go in and
what should not in an obligatory memorial issue of
presença (along with vague plans for a biography).
As for the 'nyms, Álvaro de Campos lingered in the
back, unnoticed and (for once) silent. A restless
Bernardo Soares did not make it, his boss denying
him his request for time off.   Dr. Ricardo Reis, long
ago lost to the wilds of Rio de Janeiro, did not hear
the news of Fernando's passing for days, if ever.

Mar. 11, 2015

Wisdom

Even hot air contains its
modicum of oxygen, though
that it does hardly matters in
the scheme of things. Too bad
that this realization comes
too late to be of much use.

Mar. 12, 2015

Being Posthumous

Fernando: Why is it that one's true
moment in the sun comes when one

can no longer see to see?
Álvaro: So that it can't hurt you.

Mar. 13, 2015

Pessoa the Flirt

When, at the age of 31, it occurred to the poet that it was high
time to start flirting, it wasn't long before he upped the ante
and decided that flirting is an art, nay, an art of the highest
order. And so, being who he was, he started, with the notes,
the sappy letters, the meetings (covert, of course), at odd times,
in odd places. He gave it his all, But then, suddenly, things
went bad (on his side, of course), so he called on his enforcer,
to get him out of his now-intolerable fix. It worked. He knew
now that flirtation was not conducive to art, the flirt no artist.

Mar. 14, 2015

At My Comparisons

There *are* thin men of Haddam
(I look whenever I go there or
just drive by on the main drag)
but not nearly as many as the
insurance man would have us
believe. No way does it come
close to the number of transfixed
agape young men of São Jorge or

that of the one-book poets walking
the Chiado *calçada* in my time.

Mar. 15, 2015

Salutatorian

When the sun is not out
it's as if it has never been.

It's no wonder it's saluted
by Caeiro—first thing, too.

Mar. 15, 2015

A Keeper

If you scatter selves like free-range chickens,
you mustn't bitch if they come home to roost.

Mar. 15, 2015

Computations

I never thought to acquire a small pocket-sized
pad to keep my finances straight. That's why
there are in that survivor, the *baú*, lists of monies
due for various necessities and encumbrances on
scraps of paper meant for lists of future projects,

just-thought-of publishing schemes, even poems,
fully realized ones or poems still-in-motion to be
picked up for a fresh look at some later time. I
could have used the services of a bookkeeper, say
Bernardo Soares, but I was never one to impose.

Mar. 18, 2015

Air Travel

Leonard Cohen has one persona—himself,
perhaps. He couldn't handle the demands of
several personas. That's a time-consuming
task, like juggling balls of a different size or
texture, Yet Leonard travels all over the world,
places Fernando has not seen with his own eyes.
Perhaps the old boy should have scored himself
a passport—one to keep handy, just in case.
Not the kind one buttoned up safely in the
breast pocket of a suit too worn to wear.

Mar. 20, 2015

A Full Plate

That's what he left behind, no, correction, a plate
that seems never ever to be deemed empty or, for
that matter, described as "wiped clean." What a
circus of mix-and-match clowns and high-wire
walks and elephants (catch 'em while you can, for

as long as you can, before they are returned to the
wild), words and scraps of lines to be culled from
the horde, ciphered, turned round and round until
they sort of patch up, and then duct-taped to last
for as long as they last. Thus the pile-up that adds
more and more to the body of work, one that will
be pruned into a memorable if flexible canon,
thus the care and feeding of a posthumous poet.

Mar. 24, 2015

More, More, and Still More Pessoa

The songwriters called them sectional introductions
devised to create a bridge in a musical between the
prosaic action of a play and the "real" song, easing
the response to what might otherwise seem to be an
abrupt break in the action of the play. Not in all its
senses or its wider implications, but so, too, might one
see the poet's overall plan. Set many hares running,
projects described, books assigned titles, tables of
contents (set in flux) listing works still in the works,
few near completion, most destined to languish in the
optative mood, with nary a hope that anyone might
live long enough (or have the energy) to bring them
them to book. How lucky, thus, to inherit a bevy of
self-reproducing workers who would bring order to the
remains, even to the point of producing materials that
the Master, in their opinion, would have without a doubt

have come up with to fulfill a reach if not a grasp. But
then there's the shibboleth about the making of books.

Apr. 6, 2015

Torre de Belém

Caress a fact and it will yield a meaning; act on a fancy
and it will wing away to parts unknown. If facts tend to
stick together and cool into place, fancies sky away beyond
the blue, shedding aspiration, disdainful of any and all utility.

Apr. 10, 2015

Os tempos mudam

It is taken as a sign of admiration for a people
(or their language) when someone or other notes
that to him or her the word for buttonhole is *house*
or *home*. Be wary, though, of one who (metaphor)
keeps a loose cuff, for soon or late, he will follow
the whistle not even a dog can hear and turn himself
right side out to curry favor in the new dispensation.

Apr. 21, 2015

Pride of Place (2)

Virtually every day I walked the Chiado, sometimes
noticing (but not always) the statues of the sitting
Poeta Chiado and the high-standing Camões stonily
confronting the skyline, rain or shine. And when it
was my time, I, too, became an effigy in the Chiado.
Lucky me, it was decided that my daily walk to work
and back to my room was tiring. So, unlike my worthy,
upstanding colleague, in bronze I was plunked into
a chair resting flush on the pavement, while even the
sitting Poeta Chiado's chair rests on a pedestal—a
modest one, to be sure, but a pedestal nevertheless.
Funny how much such things matter when you're gone.

Apr. 24, 2015

The Habit

will keep you going—smoking, drinking, imagining sex,
writing, obsessing (over what does not matter)—it keeps you
getting on with getting on (you hope). In crises habits are of
little use; they will continue to do their thing but will no longer
matter. No wonder that there are those who pray for crises,
whose fear is that, unawares, they have already exhausted their
portion, forgetting, of course, the truth in the saying that *quem
espera por sapatos de defunto, toda a vida anda descalço*.

Apr. 26, 2015

First Things, Last Things

The first thing Caeiro did on the last day, the poet
tells us, was greet the sun. That the poet Berryman
smiled at someone or something when he jumped
is also said, though no one can say for sure.

Apr. 30, 2015

At Random

Old women talk dirty.
They have always done
so, even when PIDE
was the law of the land.
Camões knew this, so
did Eça, and everyone
else. But it was only
oral, this license, never
internal, never written.
And now the Pope will
come to join the *fête* at
Fatima where smoke is
the rage but there's no
smoking or bare arms or
other sundry *besteiras*.
*Havia a PIDE, mas
havia respeito—vox
populi* (overheard).

May 1, 2015

Epitaph

He did not want to call undue attention
to himself, but he did want to be noticed.

May 2, 2015

Who's Afraid of Franz Kafka?

Has the book been written in which
the bug awakens to find that it has been
transformed into a human being? So,
self-congratulatory beings what they
are, how long must we pretend to be
appalled at a cheeky Czech's *blague*?

May 5, 2015

Goldilocks' Choice

So that's the key.
It's the short, pithy
poem that stays in
the memory of the
folk, though the
folk will profess
a stronger liking
for the stretched-
out performance,

the sequenced
portions of the
ode. True, the
catchy extract
will do for the
obligatory citing
but in its completion
in short compass,
with no context
to be taken into
account, it wins
out in the end,
making it
comfortably
onto a plaque
in bronze
that looks
right. Proof
that in its
discretion
it obscures
its modesty.

May 25, 2015

Mapping

Narrow
unjustified
texts tend
to mirror-

image the
shape of
my nation.
See it?

May 26, 2015

Kicking Against the Pricks

If Isabel truly was a Muse to
two giants of modern writing
(both disciples of the Master),
certainly I am not the one to
say. Moreover, beyond the fact
that she lived first with Gaspar
and then with José, I know
nothing. Nor did I ever talk
to her or even, for that matter,
meet her, though twice, we were
in the same hall, at different
Pessoa conferences held
at the Gulbenkian. The first
time, at a distance she and
José, who were, I knew, no
longer together, were at each
other's throats over something
I know not what. Years later,
I witnessed her intervention,
a passionate statement calling
for justice to Gaspar for his
magisterial achievements,

contributions that theorists
had kicked to the curb.

May 31, 2015

Semi-anonym

I'd say in 2015 that Côrtes-Rodrigues is the forgotten
one among the men of *Orpheu*, though I'm aware that
an argument can be made for Luís de Montalvor, Ronald
de Carvalho or even Antonio Ferro as a candidate for
this dubious distinction. But the fact remains, despite
the existence of his correspondence with Pessoa, that
this son of São Miguel pretty much gave up his pursuit
of Art to devote his last several decades to the least of
Modernism's tasks—writing down the words of the folk.
Montalvor became the posthumous Pessoa's publisher;
the Brazilian worked his way up in Itamaraty; Ferro
gambled on Culture even as he took up Salazar's cause.
No, it's Côrtes-Rodrigues who best fills the bill as
Orpheu's fifth Beatle. Pencil him in. Use a pen.

June 2, 2015

The Poet, the Work, the Pest

Surely an increasing number must have it,
this disease that will not go away, be cured,
or cut short its duration. People will sit on
the chair in the homage-cum-advert, shilling

for the café it fronts; or, if they be so lucky,
to charm a compliant waiter, sit upright at his
table at the Martinho da Arcada and sip from
what they will tell you is his very cup. Well,
so goes the claim, and if the claim fails to stand
up to even casual consideration, it still beats
peering beady-eyed into a glass-covered *baú*
(if you will) featuring the bones of a saint in
a bootless, teary-eyed attempt to do Time in

July 13, 2015

Fate and Fatigue

This, too, is a *baú*, a trunk, a box, a container,
metaphorically speaking, of course, even though
the texts are dated, laid out neatly, and stacked
in sequence awaiting their readers, whoever
they might turn out to be. Let the chips fall.

July 19, 2015

broken wrist

one-finger typing
no need for capitals
no need for periods
no need for commas

Aug. 15, 2015

Parabens 2

Bad politics drove Dr. Reis to the wilds of Rio,
but it was Campos who found there a lover though
he never once set foot in a land that the Portuguese
first dubbed Vera Cruz. Moreover, that lover never
made her love known to him, telling it to the world
(or, more exactly to those who had ears to agree).
By then her husband had died and so had Álvaro.
Of course she chose him over Himself. Everybody
did, after all. He scarcely noticed but it registered.
She is 99 today, and, like Niemeyer, she won't die.

Aug. 28, 2015

At the Last

He wrote that posterity will sooner than later
winnow away for remembrance even a great
poet's choice down to a generous 6 or fewer.
Sanguine in his hard-hearted prediction was
he, for even the 6 will survive but as memes.
The whole world knows no one will resist a
race to the inner space of the least in nested
dolls, standing there, standing small for all.

Sept. 1, 2015

Sand Pile

Neruda saw globes in the mix.
Blake saw eternity in a grain.
Caeiro saw it as a pile of sand.
The engineer saw it as mineral,
of course, while Dr. Reis saw
it not at all. I? I saw it shimmer
into a simile, and ran with it.

Sept. 2, 2015

Petrichor (noun)

—the smell of earth after rain—
a word he himself did not know
about something that escaped his
notice as well as (and this may
surprise) Caeiro's militant rants.

Sept. 4, 2015

Endgame

One long century after Lisbon's first snark attacks on
Orpheu there appears *O Essencial de Fernando Pessoa*
—everything the reader needs to know, in nine self-

sufficient volumes. What remains of his leavings
(a surmise) shall be left to rot away in the *baú*.

Oct. 3, 2015

Tea Leaves

"I saw him once, sitting alone in the corner of a café,
a timid soul obviously, not much worth talking about."
This was part of the small talk by Fernando Pires de
Lima, the doctor-ethnographer, well settled in Porto
and totally at home in his folk-life museum. The time
was summer 1972 or thereabouts, two or three years
before the advent of the Carnations. I told him about
the damage and boarding-up of a small museum in
Lisbon that I had noticed while riding by in a taxi.
He made a face of disgust, not having heard of this
latest bombing but showing fear for his government.
He had not a thing to say about Pessoa's writing.

Oct. 10, 2015

So It Goes

His wants were few, everybody noticed,
as he went from firm to firm, hoping
to find a bit of work, half-hoping there
would be none so he could put the office
Remington to his own use. He wanted to
go to London but didn't ever get there. He

had plans for sometimes useful inventions,
including a typewriter that would handle
translation, a publishing house where he
could issue books and pamphlets by him-
self and his friends (but this project soon
failed), translations of Shakespeare, a play
a month until he had exhausted the canon.
No, actually his wants were ever so many,
and they were large, but they languished
and died away in the hopper that is life.

Oct. 11, 2015

O intrudo, à americana

He knew about Halloween in America
and was not impressed, certainly not
favorably. Costumes and candy and
masks and bandanas, kids running about,
in groups or alone, knocking on doors,
shouting *trick or treat!*, then coming
back later, surreptitiously, to knock
over ash cans, cut clotheslines, soap
windows, no, all that fake saturnalia,
that programmed dionysianism, could
only discourage him. In a moment of
outrage he had even written down a
few words, but never saw them again.

Oct. 25, 2015

Bottoming Out

Slicing and dicing at will, they'll make
a book out of whatever pops up.

Quinto Imperio, the Masons, catty
chat anent women, etc., etc., etc.

Maybe what we need now is a break or
maybe a list of topics he never got to.

Oct. 26, 2015

Campos Says

Xarope. Now that word calls for a
word. It's like holy water. You take
as much of it as you want. An English
speaker might hear in it an imperative.

Oct. 28, 2015

The Author Laments

So many people know what I had in mind (or
would have had, had I lived) for my projected
Livro do Desassossego (if I didn't change my
mind about its title) in its final form—how else
to explain its many published versions—that I
hesitate to say that it exists only as a mass

of scattered notes toward something that I,
too, never really understood. Put it this way.
It has become something of a child's contest
where everyone gets a prize for showing up.

Oct. 30, 2015

Modernismo

I'd put up two bits
to learn that the poet
set down his immortal
lines, knowing full well
that a stone is a stein,
and that stein calls
herself Gertrude.

Oct. 31, 2015

Snuffed in Paris

Of course it was unthinkable then that one might even consider
that he might need forgiving for the solipsistic act of taking his
life. But now, on the cusp of a century later, thoughts and
memories come to the fore, and the notion persists in my
consciousness. Since he had made sure that his friends knew
all about the certainty that when the time was right he would do
it, the *fait accompli* was surprising and not surprising. Sure he
was, that they would notice from afar when he set out on the
great adventure of his life, certain that his act would change

them in ways that sometimes matter. Sweet, egregious boy.
He (and we) should at the very least have known better.

Nov. 2, 2015

Agua Benta

> Lying and deception have never had the stigma
> attached to them in the Mediterranean that they
> have in the Protestant north.
>   Gabriel Josipovici, *On Trust*

Lying? Harsh. Bending the truth, white lies, prevarication,
a joke to slip the yoke, such bits we stand guilty of and pretend,
humanly, to ignore in others. Be what it may, I prefer to mask,
you know, put on a face, letting it all go, forfeiting my right to
clamber up the side of a high horse to perseverate. It's action
that entertains as it sidetracks. So much do we hide, to divert
attention away from something or other, to save face, to find
the easy way out. Me? I went a step or two farther. I hid my
mask by masking it with still another one chosen with care.

Nov. 9, 2015

Facebook

Triumphantly add the recognizable colors to your profile
picture to show your sympathy (closely related to hatred)
for the worthy cause, the tragedy, the scandal, the shocking
surprise. It never fails. It's the ultimate joiner's trick for

as long as attention lasts. If time is of the essence though,
a quick *like* will soothe the cranky conscience of a player.

Nov. 14, 2015

Resolved

One day I'll read through this hoard of small thoughts
from start to late, weed out some, rearrange others, and
bring the whole shebang to finale. Someday, not today.
Probably never is more like it, self-love being what it is,
not to mention the need to create one more bootless list.

Nov. 16, 2015

Humm

Via face-book comes the notice that the 80th year of
the poet's demise will be marked by a reading of his
poems to be held at the Livraria Ferin but sponsored
by the Associação Portuguesa de Escritores. Reminds
me of what Groucho said about membership in clubs.

Nov. 23, 2015

Painterly Guile

Now take the Negreiros portrait, the one
done for the Irmãos Unidos restaurant
and the other one commissioned by those
at the Gulbenkian. Of course I am only
the occasion for Negreiros to foist his
brand of surrealism on the viewer. But
credit him with having captured the gap
when I shifted from haunch to haunch
(then keeping the secret a secret so long
as the likenesses were not shown side
by side. Doubtless, I over-read.

Nov. 26, 2015

Family Matter

So my niece turns ninety and remembers
fondly *o tio,* gifter of *carinhos,* small
presents I hid under the supper napkin.
Her mother, a poet's sister, inherited the
care of the trunk when I passed away,
but she never let anyone in the family
take even a peek inside. When officials
arrived, my niece recalls, they made a
mess of things. She humble-boasts that
she, too, has written books, forgetting to
recall, of course, that publishing books

(or even getting them written) was not
at all, needless to say, her uncle's forte.

Nov. 30, 2015

Karma

There are prizes now bearing my name that had
they existed in the day would never have gone
to me. Of course, it would have been my fault.
I would have to shoulder the blame for lacking
the wit to curry favor with the right ones in the
right places. But, hey, Karma is Karma, and no
matter how it works, it never comes too late.

Dec. 11, 2015

Pipe Dreams

Now trolling is something I would have done
had the internet been around in my day. And,
of course, I would have kept close track of my
enemies, though I would have been chary with
my own postings. *Word* would have helped,
too, for quiet composition, labeling folders,
squirreling away poems and unsent screeds in
files. I could also have eliminated repetition,
notably in the *desassossego* mélange, which,
come to think of it, would have cost me my
current worldwide reputation as artist and

thinker. Still, however, as Cash Bundren
puts it, it would have made for a neater job.

Dec. 14, 2015

A Life

Ferro was the youngest and non-collaborating
member of the original *Orpheu* group. Too
young legally to bear the official burden we
saddled him with, he soon went on to carve
out a career in journalism, while striking out
in the arts with his own raids into Portuguese
Modernism. But when he discovered fascism
and interviewed the leaders of such persuasion
throughout Europe, although he only faintly
discerned it, he was preparing for his tryst with
Salazar. He repurposed this sedentary professor
as a man of action by showing him looking
out at Lisbon standing beside the car that took
him to the highest of places, locales to which
they had motored in short hops by stages. The
rest is history. He titled his last book *Saudades
de Mim* (echoing, I take it, our friend Mário).
It could just as soon have been called, as I see
it, *An Unlived Life* or *Road Not Taken*.

Dec. 14, 2015

Alpha Poet

Robert Frost, an alpha poet if there ever was one
(with knowing nods to Homer and Virgil, that is),
said once to one of my follower's friends that men
are equal, they put their pants on, one leg at a time.
That's it? I could ask how it's done in Paris, but
no, it would get me laughed right out of court.

Dec. 15, 2015

Cash Cow 2

Some say he saved too much,
others not enough. Like the
Belle of Amherst, he repurposed
old envelopes and seems to have
thrown nothing away. And yet,
when they say, as they did twenty
years ago, *tanto Pessoa já enjoa,*
they were not doubling down in a
complaint about the stuff in a trunk.

Dec. 17, 2015

Proffered Advice

Housman told Terrence that it was
stupid stuff, but kept on writing
his poetry. And so did I. But now,

mon petit, you've gone too far. Can
you not write about anything else? Or
if poetry has been your compulsion,
why not try something else—a novel,
say, or, at your age, a memoir or an
autobiography, a book to be proud
of but no one will crack? Habits
die hard, because they are useful.

Dec. 17, 2015

Picture-taking

Mira the photo of the poet *en famille* or
such *famille* as he could latch onto, his
left hand resting on his niece's shoulder,
his right arm hanging on to a cigarette.

Dec. 18, 2015

Stations of the Metro

Packages don't sit! said the subway
patron to the young passenger whose
seat she coveted but didn't manage
to get. I never rode the New York
trains so this doesn't apply to me.
And I never saw the arts station of
the Lisbon metro that applies to me.

Then there is this *cara* Pomar, whose
 lines distort faces and efface walls.

Dec. 19, 2015

Creature Comforts

He never had a dog, not as a child, and certainly
not as an adult. Maybe that's what he lacked, a
creature to walk beside him down to school in
Durban, later in the Chiado by the Bertrand, a
creature to keep him company in his room nights.
He might have written less were he not alone,
maybe more. My god, of all the thoughts to have.
Such thoughts kept him from Ofélia, twice, thank
God. The caged raven at the *galego*'s bar was
chanticleer enough for him. *Chanté! Chanté!*

Dec. 20, 2015

Roosters

Never attending the *missa do galo* in the church
of my village, for instance, or singing the praises
of the soupy queen who escaped the king's wrath
by showing him a shower of roses or by tooting
boundless praise for the bounties of the plucky
galo de Barcelos—I could say I could go on.

Dec. 22, 2015

Cansaço

Mental fatigue is sort of like the body's metal fatigue.
Seldom before the crash is there true detection. What's
left is a gabardine, two pullovers, two ties, an old suit
that penuriously one thinks might someday be put back
into emergency use, pairs of shoes and slippers (one pair
each), two or three typewriter ribbon cartridges (lifted
from the wastebasket at work), and a penknife, employed
mainly to sharpen pencil stubs varied in color. Oh, I for-
got the three shirts (their number an extravagance) and an
umbrella (carried every day to the *Baixa*, just in case).

Dec. 29, 2015

Revenants

I leave behind no -ex, unless Ofélia counts.
I did have loyalties, affiliations really, fewer,
though, than people think. I was born a loner,
one who clings to imagined cronies, of the
kind, you know, who cast shadows over me.

Dec. 29, 2015

Before E-mail

He left behind a trunk but no money to pay
the rent, which was in arrears. There was no
one to redeem the situation, so the landlord

kept the trunk. This took place years ago.
Thus did my letters to Sá-Carneiro disappear.
All editions, old or new, tell the same tale.

Dec. 30, 2015

Hail and Farewell

On this day, the last of the year, I find that
I have nothing to say, beyond wishing myself

a sane, healthy, prosperous 2016. That's it.
But at the moment I still have 12 hours to go.

Well nothing has occurred to me in that time,
so I turn to the start of my next year, hoping

for inspiration, something other than the act
of adding, clumsily, the date to my date-line.

Grouse: there's an increase in the need for
mirrors when there's no urge to use them.

Dec. 31, 2015 / Jan. 1, 2016

Morpheus to Freud

Nod off, and the
mind will cavort.
Now do your thing.

Jan. 2, 2016

Alas

To be left to one's own devices
fosters anxiety and, sometimes,
creativity. But don't count on it.
Kidney stones are more like it.

Jan. 5, 2016

In Character

Not the power pose but some-
thing like its opposite. For some
this would have been a bane. For
me it was a blessing, or at least as
much of a blessing as I would ever
receive. As for Caeiro and Campos,
they would have been nothing if
not for the pose: Alberto is always
sure of himself in every situation,
Álvaro mainly so. Reis? a more
complex case, so quick is he with

shibboleths of doom and gloom.
Oh, to have had the courage of
a Botto or the brio of a Bowie!

Jan. 6, 2016

Take It From Me

The imposter syndrome says never,
ever be *in situ*, never, ever be caught
off or on guard. Never, ever cast a
catchable or even, if you can manage
it, a discernible halo, aura, or shadow.
Otherwise, be true to yourself.

Jan. 8, 2016

Tracks

I must check the Brazilian census.
I don't know what became of him
after he left his own native land in
a huff over the chaos created by the
republicans. Still, I'm not even sure
that he found life more palatable in
the land of Vera Cruz, such that he
might settle down and write his

usual litanies of kvetch and doom.
No doubt about it, I must check.

Jan. 9, 2016

Rain in Lisbon

Dia de chuva, dia de pancadaria,
as the woman liked to say, repeating
her mother's saying. Well, it is not
quite that, but the rain does beat
down on this Sunday beneath a seam-
less gray sky, and it's just three weeks
into what will be a long winter. But
there are no kids around, so it's up
to me to beat up on myself. They
say this heavy rain is good for the
soil, for the next crop, but here we
have no farmers if we discount the
jardinière, that is, the one who on
the least sunny of sunny days will
put out a pot of choice geraniums.

Jan. 10, 2016

Big Walt

Nobody saw it coming when he gave up journalism
for poetry. But no doubt, it was a seismic shift. He
dropped the comparative at the end of his given name

and relished the one-syllable name he would blare out
for the next forty years. Walt, he insisted, contained
multitudes, though he was too confident in what he
had done to take the time to baptize each or even one.
Too greedy in his grab to let things fall as they may,
he swallowed his multitudes whole. It was a lesson.

Jan. 11, 2016

Attributions

You'd never know that he had a bedroom with
a view of the street and, of course, a shade to
keep out the dark. His night world was all paper
and a pen. There he could indulge in lubrications
that came to him right off but not always clearly
assigned. Hence the question mark, occasionally,
after the initials A. C. or R. R. on a poem. Almada
alone saw them decked out, faces to meet the day.

Jan. 12, 2016

No Jack, No

On this, the umpteenth birthday of the inventor of
the literary Klondike, I am reminded anew that I can-
not read in books or stories anything of the hard hard-
ships of man or dog in the midst of terrible cold and
even more terrible wind. No, it's not for me, I who

shiver in my shoes when weather turns in the Chiado
and the rain begins to drip from the brim of my hat.

Jan. 12, 2016

Binary

I should be grateful to her cousin, who, after my
death in 1935, took to the radio to extol my work
and to explain my life. So doing, he scotched
rumors about my sexuality. He let the genie out
of the bottle, in an age of either/or, about my head-
over-heels infatuation with his then young cousin
at the firm. His bio truth took center stage and
held sway, until the skeptics said, *Yes, but...*

Jan. 14, 2016

The Doodle

I sing of the demise of the doodle, extinct as the
dodo, wiped out at the hands, so to speak, of the
computer screen. No need now to find paper or
pad for the sake of any sort of composition, when
composition on the screen is uniform in its signs
and symbols or emoticons. There may still be a
surprise or two in store but, if so, they'll tap into
another part of the brain. Pure backsliding, I say.

Jan. 15, 2016

After Camus

Sisyphus could not move mountains.
He couldn't even push one rock and
have it stay put. But he tried, and he
tried, and that's his portion of grit.
There are many kinds of rock, not all
of them mineral. And like hats, the
one comes in all sizes, in most colors.
Take, for instance, the great molasses
flood that inundated Boston a century
ago, halting only when good and ready.
Well, that's not a convincing example
—after all, Sisyphus set a standard—
but I bet you get what I'm getting at.

Jan. 16, 2016

Campos Ruminates

> *Dia de São Martinho*
> *mata o teu porquinho.*

He knew the saying, not the ritual.
Whether it should be *teu* or *seu*, he
sometimes wondered, but that's as
far as his interest took him. His
taste, like his interest, was turned
seaward, toward *sardinhas, carapau,*
 and the ubiquitous *bacalhau.* It did
not conjure up memories of festive

matanças, washing casings, stuffing
them with pork to make *chouriços*,
bread to make *farinheiras*, saving
every drop of blood for *morcelas*—
too far back in the annals of his family
to evoke nostalgia, a sentiment. He
did fancy *dobrada á moda do Porto*,
though he never could get over that time
when his serving was served up to him,
not hot, as it must be, but cold—like
revenge. Nothing to do. Pay the piper.

Jan. 17, 2016

Abel's

One came to Abel's for drink. The olives on a plate
set out on the bar lay untouched by the regulars.
Dawdling was permitted but not condoned, at times
discouraged by Abel's actions, such as lifting a slow
drinker's glass, wiping the spot, then setting the glass
down slowly. Privy to the practice, the regulars drank
their drinks at one gulp, much like the Russian drinks
vodka. Playing within defined bounds, a place lasts.

Jan. 18, 2016

The Jennings Papers

It's another case of *o portugues não faz
e não deixa fazer*, this matter of how the
Hubert Jennings papers did not wind up
at the Biblioteca Nacional. Whatever the
reason, from head or heart (not for money),
the South African's heirs chose elsewhere.

Jan. 18, 2016

Vital Signs

On workdays I never felt the full bone-chill tremor
that, like clockwork, between 1 and 2 o'clock, came
upon me on Sundays and holidays. It would pass
away in due time, and then I would wonder about it,
reprising the anecdote of the old man who after his
terrible thirst was slaked, could not let go of the
memory, and continued his grouse to all within sight.

Jan. 18, 2016

Confederacy

To start hares that are still running
is no mean feat, and, by hook and
by crook, I did that. The problem
is that the hunter (man or dog) has
not much choice in this matter,

and must take what comes. It's
just a matter of guns and roses.

Jan. 19, 2016

It's Always About Me

New York is accessibility to experience was
said by Marianne Moore, the librarian-poet
famous for larger-than-life hats. To mind
comes the one that she would not take off
even to have her picture taken with the Sit-
wells at the Gotham Book Mart (now gone)
where a sign outside humble-boasted that this
was the place where wise men came to fish.
To me, Lisbon was my access to experience,
though my circuit even in that small place was
only habitual and intentionally circumscribed.
Fortunately, my boys could go where I feared
to go. Yet while America lay to the west, and
Paris to the northeast, they limited themselves
to drives up the road to Sintra (though, much
like Kafka's doctor, they never got there). Even
I, who went once to Portalegre to buy a printing
press, wrote nothing on the trip until the train
was chugging along to the station at Santa
Apolónia. Or was it the Rossio station?

Jan. 21, 2016

Lithotripsy

It was said that I died from some sort of kidney
disease. Fortunately, I was never diagnosed as
suffering from kidney stones, lumps formed of
minerals in urine and caused by eating meat and
drinking red wine. Meat I ate little of, but red
wine was an entirely different matter. While my
kidneys did not form stones, at least not any that
caused problems, there were other body formations,
I suspect, that I could have done without. Those
were in my brain and there was no laser shockwave
to smash them to pieces. In *my* head, I tell you.

Jan. 22, 2016

Due Diligence

Sonnets he wrote to show that he could do
them. They were arrows bending swiftly
to the center of a distant target or the one-
two-three rapid-shots piercing cans tossed
into the air for the purpose. Disposables,
such poems meant nothing to him. Even
the Barrow-on-Furness series was merely
casual work, work done with the left hand.

Jan. 23, 2016

First Responders

What expectations did they have when they
answered the call to check for the hidden fire
that might or might not be there, dangerous
in the layers of packed trash in a dumpster?
Would they find buried gold, real gold, or
merely fool's' gold, the mock? Or worse,
heaps of trash that not even the most assiduous
of pickers would not salvage? They would see
the lay of the land, pick out some of what they
chose to call nuggets and rush into print. Of
course, the poet-scholar who later, much later,
ventured to say that everything worth its sale
had already been put into print by the man
himself in his lifetime. But who could assess
such notions until after the dump—a legacy—
had been picked clean? The cleanup goes on.

Jan. 25, 2016 / Apr. 12, 2016

Canto a Galicia

There's a bookstore in the old part
of Santiago de Compostela that sells
books that are portuguese or galician.
Nothing *castelhano*. Nothing at all.
It's a political thing; his stock high..

Jan. 26, 2016

Art

Thanks to the scratches on the *Faculdade*
wall, we all know what the three of them
look like; but we do not know how, in
full flower, they appeared to the poet in
his mind's eye (though he did supply his
credulous follower with identity-card
details in a fulsome screed, knowing all
would be cherished and squirreled away).
One wonders, naturally, how Himself
might have reacted to those many other
of his biographical constructs, let alone,
of course, the fourth figure on the wall,
spread-eagled before a presumed sky?
Jennings saw him as *the poet of many
faces*. He left no sketches to show us.

Jan. 27, 2016

The Wheel Turns

Announce *inéditos* at a certain point in the
poet's posthumous career and it will spark
chamas. Once again the poet has put out,
though seldom has the unburied "new"
revised readers' views regardless of the
pitch now piped. *Au contraire*, such texts
have served, at best, to reaffirm what every-

body always knew. Thankful they are, that
at least the quality hasn't dropped by much.
.

Jan. 28, 2016

Forgive Me

As we get close to half a thousand of these things,
I, yes I, have reached the conclusion that there
is too much *I* in them, way too much *I* in these pages.
And I should know, as the inventor of that myriad
myriad of different selves that the world has called
personages, assumed, sometimes, for a moment, an
hour, others for the duration and beyond. Good,
isn't it, to be both the penitent and the confessor.

Jan. 31, 2016

Star Wars e o Boule

Pride and prejudice, yes, but sense
and sensibility, not a whiff. The *Star
Wars* shibboleth *may the Force be
with you* and the morning greeting
como vão essas forças? may be no
more than kissing cousins, and thus
it ends right here. Lucas, an only child,
was born in Modesto, which reminds
me, for some reason, of the historian—
his delight when, stepping off the bus,

he spotted a squirrel on the campus in
Nashville, and squealed, *um esquilo*!
It was as if he'd never seen one before.

Jan. 31, 2016

Obras de Mafra

Luciana knew her onions. That's why they
went to her first. She knew Lisbon as only
she, an outsider, could know the city. She
could peel the onion that wasn't Fernando
down to the nothing that was. Replace her
with know-nothings and ask them to deliver
results. Start out clean, start out ignorant,
with feigned interest, a show of curiosity
fit for an Englishman. *Paga e não bufa.*

Feb. 1, 2016

Sounds of Sound

The moving shadows of birds that flew
between me and the sun are a comfort
to me as I walk the Rua dos Douradores.
Noiseless, they nothing mean beyond
themselves. The sudden bolt across the
sky, however, is another thing altogether.
It casts no shadow but is followed, at
close intervals, by claps of thunder. No

wonder Walt advised future generations
to look for him under their boot soles.
It takes all that I can do not to scream,
soundlessly, like the spastic ninny of
Munch's painting, the one who, at his
back, hears explosions of thunder.

Feb. 2, 2016

Country Western Song

I cherish not the train song. Our train ran
out to Oeiras and beyond, and that was the
end of it. In actuality I never wanted to get
out of town at all so train toots and signals
meant nothing useful to me. They were
there for lonely people on lonely ranches
in a cowboy movie, fancying long whistles
fading into the dark. Not my thing. Those
librarians in Cascais saw right through me.

Feb. 5, 2016

Wit or Wisdom?

*O que se come e bebe é o melhor que se leva
deste mundo,* my mother used to say. Maybe so.
For some people, but not me. Oh yes, drink had
a special place in my days and nights, but food
only when it could serve me allegorically in a

poem. Always, lunchtime meant a drink or two,
and dinner, a sit-down affair, the penance for an
earlier drink, but earnest for the drink to come.

Feb. 6, 2016

The Stage Was Paris

Our man in Paris was a one-trick pony.
At the last I came to realize that. His
choice of subjects was always himself.
Self-centered brat, he thought he had
invented a way to *épater la bourgeoisie.*
Yet he couldn't find enemies who would
read him for they knew him not at all,
and his streetwalkers, who kept him in
petty cash, cared not a fig. As they say
in show business, his death was a good
career move. I'm relieved my side of
the mail, packed away for safe-keeping
in a trunk, was lost when the trunk
itself vanished. Finders keepers, I
always say, but never losers weepers.

Feb. 7, 2016

Supply-side

I wonder what the *livrarias* would
set out in their *montras*, what books,

mute, their covers facing outward
to capture the attention of those who
stop to stare or those, hurrying along,
who register automatically the message:
Buy! Buy! In Lisbon, Porto, Coimbra,
window displays revel in the latest
Pessoa book (by or about), a sure
sign that all's right in his world.

Feb. 10, 2016

Ofélia e Nininho

Move what remains to Prazeres so
that she will now lay a bit closer.
It does not matter, I suppose, that
he himself was retrieved, with an
over-plus of fanfare, and planted
in the courtyard at Jerónimos,
close to (but not hard by) those
catafalques of Camões and Gama.
History, as it's writ, is a tchoky.

Feb. 14, 2016.

What If

How different it could have been
had Luciana or Teresa Rita Lopes
taken charge of bringing the papers

to book. But alas it was not to be.
They knew too much and were,
ipso facto, not right for the job.
Devoid of expertise in the matter
at hand, the philologist was put in
charge, and in charge he is to this
day, routinely releasing volumes,
predicated on notes, not always in-
dispensable.

Feb. 19, 2016

Doctors Do Not Self-Diagnose

He was so adept at casting horoscopes,
entries into the future, calculations to
the moment for even his imaginary folk,
that the great magus, Aleister Crowley,
crossed the straits to see for himself.
Odd, then, that an error in casting his
own fortune should have promised him
more life than he would ever see.

Feb. 19, 2016

A Tale of Two Cities

The weather was good, the day sunny,
just as the forecaster had said. It was a
good day for photography, and he was

out, on the lookout. To keep in practice,
perhaps, he snapped one of the foreign-
language business correspondent, stepping
smartly along to meet a commitment, to
write that letter and catch the post. Note
that he carries no umbrella, a choice Mike,
his half-brother, off in London, would not
condone. Do not picture this *alfacinha* in
bowler, dangling a jet black, rolled-up
guarda chuva, tied back, but at the ready.
A dour man made even more dour by life
in sticky weather, pitching poems of mist.

Feb. 22, 2016

Refuse

What did he do with the scraps
that from the get-go did not pass
muster? He certainly didn't leave
them for the sweeper. Perhaps he
hid them in the pockets of the suit
he would wear that day. No one
would look into the wastebasket
at work (certainly not the janitor)
for scraps in a foreign script.

Feb. 24, 2016

Three's the Charm

Before there was Prosac or Valium or
even Miltown, he could write nothing
but words for the *calhamaço* the world
would come to know as *The Book of
Disquiet*. Hemingway, who was among
the multitudes who suffer from the same
malady, named it, it will be recalled, the
black ass, and drank and drank and
drank more and more whiskey, to little
avail. But now here's a question. What
do you do when they tell you the whole
shebang is waffled together from three
distinguishable texts? Turn one into a
triptych. *Voila!* Thrice the glory.

Feb. 25, 2016

How It Went Down

Unable to feel emotions that I sensed
the others were feeling, I projected my-
self into those others of my own making
who would feel for me. They would
enact to my benefit the life experiences
played out around me. Thus I'd never
have to miss everything and, in a way,
have my own portion of life. I took up
the word *heteronomia* to lend heft to
those patsies I gifted with words. Who

was I to intervene in their lives, those who
respect not me but only what they know?

Feb. 27, 2016

Fixing the Narrative

Asked for info on
when and how he
came to *heteronomia*,
he recalled the date
—the exact date. It
surprises still that he
didn't pin it down to
the minute, nay, to a
nanosecond. Sure,
he could have done it,
but my notion is that
had he done so, it'd
have proved to be a
tad TMI to lay on his
snippy acolyte. It's not
that what I think at all
matters, I know, but I
have a hunch that he
made up the tale of a
red-letter day, not out
of whole cloth, I will
allow, but as a self-
serving layer of thick

description, you know,
as in Clifford Geertz.

Feb. 29, 2016

Grin and Bear It

Somebody's bitching because there's
now a ten-euro charge to set foot in
the great tomb that is Jerónimos. I
guess they must be charging for Gama
and Camões as well. Pay for Prazeres?
Not so much.

Mar. 4, 2016

The Alliance

When in 1916 Germany declared war
on Portugal, a rival for African colonies,
Portugal set about assembling an army
for trench warfare in France, but it was
in no rush. Eventually, however, it sent
its people there to be killed. I know this
because seventy-five years ago I saw a
movie, *João Ratão*, which tells it like it
is. Vasco Santana never lies. See for
yourself. You must find it. YouTube.

Mar. 4, 2016

O tudo e o nada

She was no Eurydice to me, nor was I
her Orpheus. Never would I have looked
back to see if she was still at my back,
following me out of Hades. Maybe that's
because I wouldn't have gone to that hell-
hole to begin with. More like Hamlet, I'd
have sent her off to a nunnery, which, of
course, is what I accomplished, some say.

Mar. 6, 2016

Talk is Not Cheap

How clever of the young poet to bring
his aunt into the memorial, quelling for
once (if not forever) those voices of the
world buzzing about in the cafes anent
the Master's proclivity. Of course he did
not do it without Ofélia's consent (to be
sure) or without a nod (I'll bet) from the
kahuna, o porta-voz do Estado Novo.

Mar. 8, 2016

Devoutly to be Desired

These days *decolonization* is hot.
Study, supported by hefty grants

in a lean season, goes on in major
European countries. Time, I say,
for a look into *depersonalization.*
Now that's a subject you can sink
your teeth into.

Mar. 11, 2016

Small Craft Warnings

He never cared for craft.
He trusted himself to strike
poems straight off. If he got
struck on a word or a rhyme,
he just left a blank to be filled
in in due time (or not at all)
and went on straight to the
end of his poem. Oh, to be
sure, once in a while he put
on his theory cap, but he was
not one to let such notions
mar a line or a poem.

Mar. 13, 2016

Short People Got No Right

Certain parts of Portugal seem to
feature diminutive men. To escape
the curse, he trotted out his big boys

all above average, just like himself.
Just like me. Wimps.

Mar 13, 2016

Deconstructionism

They toiled and they roiled to see what
the word was hiding, doing it all for its
own sake, showing off their results little
Jack Horner-like in his corner with nary
a plum to bite. On the other hand, ever
cognizant of this unruly roil but faithful
to his faith that it would always come to
head for those with the head to see it, he
set free each word to do its work.

Mar. 21, 2016

One for the Team

Right off, from the get-go they made clear that they
were not minions, at least not mine, that Caeiro would
stick like glue to his one theme, that Reis, his nose in
the air even then, was too firmly set in his ways to
consider or even entertain the notion that he might do
something different, the engineer, whose ants-in-the-
pants make-up made him sometimes useful but was

always too unpredictable for confidence—in short I
could count on him to do it, but always his way. The
engineer and I fought at times. Take *Tabacaria*, done
in my voice, clearly, but which he so liked that I could
do nothing but fork it over. Other times, not a one
would touch a poem with a ten foot pole. So I had to
swallow hard before assuming ownership, such being
the case with *O poeta é um fingidor*, a signature poem
for me, it turned out, but that none of them ever had
the decency to acknowledge, let alone congratulate
me, in that one instance, on my extraordinary luck.

Mar. 27, 2016

Advice

Not again will you see the sonnet
wrapped tight into the Rumford
Baking Powder can and dropped
into water where a river meets
the sea. Best to keep a copy.

Apr. 10, 2016

About the Author

George Monteiro has taught English and Portuguese Studies at Brown University. He maintains interests in the areas of English-language and Portuguese-language literature and culture. In addition to *The Coffee Exchange* and *Double Weaver's Knot*, books of poetry, he has published critical studies of Henry James, Stephen Crane, Ernest Hemingway, Robert Frost, Elizabeth Bishop, Luis de Camões, and Fernando Pessoa, as well as translations of the poetry of Jorge de Sena, Miguel Torga, Pedro da Silveira, and Fernando Pessoa, and the prose of José Rodrigues Miguéis and José Saramago. He and his wife, Brenda Murphy, make their home in Connecticut.

www.ingramcontent.com/pod-product-compliance
Lightning Source LLC
Chambersburg PA
CBHW020224180626
46810CB00006B/2035